CW00840190

From Helmand to Heywood

Des Farry

DEDICATION

Dedicated to everyone, particularly those who have already read the first short version who see and enjoy the funny side of life through the prism of black humour in *Did Socrates Get Pissed?* Following requests for a follow up, DSGP? has been expanded into *From Helmand to Heywood* to meet these requests. If you don't fit this profile then read no further this book is NOT for you.

First published in Great Britain by FBS Wanderscan Ltd

Review extracts of Did Socrates Get Pissed?

Amazon.uk If you've ever wondered how Diamond In, Diamond Out and toy helicopters can be used to catch Guardian readers – then this is the book for you. Des Farry has created some great laugh out loud moments, as Fred, Chardonnay, Royston, Darren, Stuart et al. get on each-others' nerves, indulge in cringe-worthy management speak and acronyms (BASSTARDS, PASTELLS, DTPECO), jump to wrong conclusions and generally get into scrapes.

Enjoyable read, Tongue in cheek, of the moment, wickedly captures the essence of those who are self- obsessed, self- indulgent, self- righteous and who go out of their way to let others know what's best for them whether they like it or not.

Great short read, looking forward to the follow up

Amazon.com This is a first class enjoyable short read written in a humorous entertaining style. It is British black comedy. It is the interplay with both colleagues and the opposite sex which allow for a lot of laughs and ends in the Lower Pennines in England where Fred has unwittingly created the UK No. 1 Dogging spot

An entertaining short story about a man with closed memory syndrome. Some chapters are very humorous, but the book quickly becomes more serious.

I loved this book and was very pleasantly surprised. It was full of intrigue and surprise. I would really recommend it as a book to read!

Reading this book reminded me of the " It's more than my jobs worth" managers that I worked alongside in the sixties. A very entertaining read.

Goodreads This is a humorous short story, very tongue in cheek, hilarious in parts.

I really enjoyed this novella.. I await the follow up with anticipation.

Great British humor. Funny short book. I enjoyed the story. If you love British humor this is a book for you.

Very, very funny! Well worth a read, especially if the weather is so gloomy outside.

A very funny dark book. Totally enjoyed after the initial start.

I laughed out loud, in public, with no shame at this story. It's great. My only fault is that it is far far, far too short.

CONTENTS

Chapter 1

TALIBAN TORA BORA

'Today, we're talking about unfortunate funny incidents caused by absent mindedness, on the show, just ring us now,' said the broadcaster, 'and tell us your story, let's see who we've got on the line.'

'It's Alan, Alan from Droylsden.'

'Alan, you're through to the *Mike Sweeney Show on BBC Radio Manchester*[1], what's your story?'

' Mike, I got talking to my wife about decorating the rear of the house last year. She agreed, decided to leave me to it and go shopping for the day to get out of the way.'

'So I got the ladders up, brushed off the loose paint on the windows and doors, climbed up and was just about to reach and hang the tin of paint on a tread when the handle broke off, the paint poured out over my head and splattered all down me.'

'I'm covered from head to toe in white paint. I think, 'I can't go back into the house like this,'

'So I strip off, wipe the paint off as best as I can and try and open the back door to get in and finish off but I can't. My wife has forgotten all about me in the back when she went shopping and has locked me out.'

'So there I am, standing bollock naked in the back yard,

---

[1] Mike Sweeney Show BBC Radio Manchester
http://www.bbc.co.uk/programmes/p0195t4s/episodes/player

bright sunshine beaming on me and the paint starts to dry. In the meantime, I'm walking around looking like Michelin Man!'

'Hahahahaha!'

'It took me about 4 weeks to get it all off.'

'Hahahaha ,great story there Alan, we're all creased here in the studio, let's see who's next on the line.'

Besharat smiled to himself and thought about how much his life had changed in the past six months he had lived in North West England.

It had been difficult for him initially when he arrived. The abrupt difference between his old life in Helmand and his new one in Heywood jarred with him.

He got depressed and felt suicidal. With no one else locally from Afghanistan to share his troubles, he rang the Samaritans,not the local branch,but the Kabul Samaritans.

Speaking in his native Pashto, he was able to confide and unburden himself of his worries and depression.

They were really interested and excited about his suicidal thoughts and asked him if he could drive a truck.

He worked his way through it all, a routine developed, and life in his new homeland started to move upward.

He had just finished another batch of food in the Afghan kitchen he had constructed using his Army Interpreter Resettlement Grant in the back yard of Nick's house for his pop up delicatessen stall in the local market.

It was his old Army patrol friend Sid who had blagged a lot of of the building materials 'off the back of a lorry' or from local new build developers' estates just down the road at Hopwood Mews, along with Fred. Fred had volunteered as a plasterer on a local Veterans' Project to provide homes for ex-servicemen loosely based on the *BBC Nick Knowles Veterans' Village Project in East Manchester*[2]. Through it he had got a load of offcuts, tiles and other useful stuff for a small build in a back yard.

Nick had built a micro-brewery for his craft beers alongside Besharat's kitchen.

It was Nick who had come up with the winning trade name and strap line for their joint food and drink business.

TALIBAN TORA BORA

Chapter 2

From Helmand to Heywood

Nick had kept up to date from Camp Bastion on emerging food and drink trends in Greater Manchester and realized that with the plethora of curry restaurants and drinking spots you needed to differentiate into a niche market to pull in the discerning punters.

His hometown of Heywood was a perfect launch spot for his and Besharat's joint venture.Straight off the M60 and M62 with low rents, only 6 miles from the City Centre, it already

---

[2] DIY SOS Veterans' Village
http://www.telegraph.co.uk/news/uknews/theroyalfamily/11942499/Fit-for-heroes-Welcome-to-Veterans-Street.html

had the best kept secret Tapas[3] and Greek[4] restaurants in Greater Manchester, a dismal High Street of samey curry and fried chicken takeaways and formerly in the Guinness Book of Records for having the most pubs in a linear mile in England, it was ripe for a new craft beer boozer and upmarket niche Eastern cuisine establishment.

He already had in mind his first two brews, Monkeytown[5] Malt and in deference to Heywood's larger close neighbouring town, Middleton Moonraker[6].

With the Single Regeneration Bid already having been long in operation and established in place as 'Heart of Heywood' and other initiatives offering the prospect of grants for new business, he started to fine tune the figures.

Both their business plan and strap line were already in place .

TALIBAN TORA BORA

Take A Look In Besharat And Nick's …Taste Our Real Abgoosht …Booze On Real Ale.

Elsewhere in the house life had started to stir. Apart from himself and Nick, Fred and Sid were also staying there.

Besharat took a drag on his cigarette, had a quick sip of his

---

[3] The Willows https://www.tripadvisor.co.uk/ShowUserReviews-g1076971-d3977856-r305344348-Willows_Gourmet_Bistro-_Rochdale_Greater_Manchester_England.html
[4] The Parthenon Taverna https://www.tripadvisor.co.uk/Restaurant_Review-g1076971-d2153843-Reviews-Parthenon_Taverna-Heywood_Rochdale_Greater_Manchester_England.html
[5] Monkey Town http://heywoodmonkey.blogspot.co.uk/2012/04/hey-hey-were-monkey-town.html
[6] Middleton Moonraker https://en.wikipedia.org/wiki/Middleton,_Greater_Manchester

hot Nescafe and looked up at the Pennines. There was still a light covering of snow on the peaks and shaded small valleys but Spring was definitely on the way.

It was a crisp early morning with a light wind slowly turning the wind turbines up on Scout Moor.[7] In a strange way the mountain view reminded him off his old home in Kabul, the mountains of Tora Bora and his job as interpreter for the patrol in Helmand.

Chapter 3

Reflections on Helmand

The view invariably led his mind to drift back to his last days in Helmand with the patrol when the message came through that the British Army was withdrawing.

Besharat stood with his back to the sun just behind the patrol who were clearing the way ahead looking for landmines and Improvised Explosive Devices (IEDs).

He knew them all well and had been their interpreter for over 6 months. They worked well together.

His job as interpreter had not been what he had in mind when he had completed his Hotel and Catering Studies with Diploma in English Course at the Bakhtar[8] Institute of Higher Education in Kabul but that now seemed such a long time ago.

He had intended to work in the External Economic Affairs Ministry (EEAM) but for that to happen you needed contacts,

---

[7] http://www.bbc.co.uk/news/uk-england-manchester-34113160 Scout Moor
[8] Bakhtar University http://www.bakhtar.edu.af/

influence and more importantly plenty of cash for bribing your way in.

To get into the EEAM with the prospect of an overseas posting to an international hotel group was a fiercely contested opportunity, a glittering prize which was currently beyond him.

It would all take time with no certainty of a successful conclusion was the advice from his University tutors who had kept their heads down ,worked through and survived the various regimes who had held power in Afghanistan.

'There are more crashed planes in the sea than there are submarines in the sky,' said his personal Tutor, summing up the difficulties and hurdles in negotiating the political minefields.

His teachers at Bakhtar had been mainly Indian and Pakistani nationals who had been trained through British Council courses and opportunities.

All of them faithfully kept abreast of world affairs and what was actually happening in Afghanistan through the BBC World Service on clandestine radios.

It was his personal Tutor who had pointed him in the direction of acting as an interpreter for the British rather than the US Army.

'Sometime soon this war will start to wind down and the British will be the first to leave. They've never wanted to be here in the first place, memories of heavy British casualties in the two Anglo Afghan wars in the 19th century still influence policy.'

'Then there was a purpose to protect British interests in

India. Now there is none, they have simply been pressganged into an impossible mission by the Americans.'

'There's already a scheme for interpreters to be resettled elsewhere in Afghanistan with a large cash grant or relocate to the UK. The Americans will be staying behind for several years because they will never learn from the British experience,' he said.

It was the best decision Besharat had ever made.

Chapter 4

End of tour of duty

The lives of both Besharat and the patrol changed forever one day during the daily inspection of both the surface and culverts on foot and in Mastiff and Jackal armoured vehicles for improvised explosive devices along Route 601 to Lashkar Gah.

That was when the Army Careers of Fred and the other patrol members came to an end.

Not immediately but phased over a few months when they had finished their tour of duty.

Fred was guarding the engineers putting in the roadside irrigation systems from the outward patrol base.

It had similarities and reminded him of allotments back home in England with wide swathes each side of the highway now producing crops of vegetables for the local farmers in an initiative to try and reduce their dependence on producing poppies for the opium trade.

It was then that the text came through.

'Following the Defence Forces' Review of manpower requirements your unit is being reduced in size and merged. As a result of this you will be made redundant in three months following your return to the United Kingdom.'

Not totally unexpected but it still came as a shock.

A career which had brought him to Northern Ireland, Belize, Germany and Cyprus was coming to an end in the dust and chaos of Helmand.

Back at Camp Bastion he confided his worries about the future to Wily Sid who was a mixture of Private Walker from *Dad's Army and Fletcher from Porridge.*[9]

'They'll probably reduce the Camp Bastion numbers through natural wastage by the Taliban or use our Allies,' he cheerfully told a startled Fred, pointing to the joke warning sign in the Mess-Danger !!! Americans Working Overhead!'

His good natured spiv character and ladies' man rolled into a cheerful wide boy who always seemed to be able to source supplies, official and unofficial with much appreciated tubes of Robert Mugabe mints to counter the Bastion dust (RM backwards is Yorkshire slang 'E Ba Gum, Trebor!) as well as solving colleagues' marital problems in their correspondence with wives and partners back in the UK.

He was the cheerful guy who always kept morale going with his black humour.

It was the Christmas visit of the Prime Minister to Bastion and his rousing speech over the turkey and chipolatas to the

---

[9] Hugely popular BBC TV Comedy Shows

troops that helped to sustain and unleash it.

'What we do for ourselves dies with us,' said the PM, 'What we do for others and the world remains and is immortal. It is the Soldier, not the poet, who has given us freedom of speech.'

A rousing Hear! Hear! and table banging from the squaddies reverberated around the Mess.

'The PM has fired us all up tonight. I think we'd all kill for the Nobel Peace Prize for him after that speech,' Sid radioed to his unit under heavy fire in Kandahar.

After the formalities the PM worked the floor, his easy social manner made conversation and contact with the squaddies relaxed.

'Call me Dave,' he announced, shaking hands all around.

He was highly approachable and even took a turn on the turntables as DJ.

'Any music requests, any favoured tracks?,' he shouted into the mike.

'Can we have the Bee Gees *Staying Alive*?,'[10] retorted Sid.

They all laughed at the black humour.

He followed it up by dragging a large box in Christmas wrapping to the top table,

'Finally got the landmine that I'd ordered on eBay, bloody expensive phew! Cost me an arm and a leg.'

---

[10] https://www.youtube.com/watch?v=I_izvAbhExY Staying Alive Bee Gees

It brought the house down.

Sid's blagging skills and innate ability to get a copy of the Sun and pass it around the base and produce quality cigars for celebrations, at a price of course, made him popular all over Bastion.

His knowledge about women had largely been cultivated from *Deidre's Photo Casebook in the Sun*.[11]

From this Sid deduced the following about women:

Women spent a lot of time in their underwear.

Women spent a lot of time on the phone.

Women cheated on their partners.

Women cheated with their friends' partners as well.

It was this philosophy which underpinned his attitudes towards women and cemented his reputation as a womaniser.

He was the oracle on relationship problems within Bastion with the right word or phrase for a letter, text or phone call home.

Fred's relationship with his partner Chardonnay was a bit like ships passing in the night. On his last leave they had a short unsuccessful break in Benidorm.

Army married life was always difficult to maintain with frequent absences through postings, specialist training and separations preventing a settled routine. By its' very nature, orders gave very little time with women expected to fall in

---

[11] Popular Advice column in leading British tabloid newspaper.

line with Army requirements, their needs and careers etc. were rarely considered. They were expected to pack up their family lives and follow their menfolk often at very short notice.

Fred had met Chardonnay at a local function . He had just joined the Army, she was a door to door sales and party organiser for Avon Calling[12].

Courtship was rapid. The wedding soon followed. Inevitably Wily Sid was his best man with a speech based on the Essence of Man Avon products.

The wedding dinner was at Fing's All You Can Eat Chinese Buffet House with a short honeymoon in York then it was straight into cramped married quarters at Catterick.

Chardonnay never really settled into Catterick, she was an urban dweller by instinct and by calling. Door to door selling and organising a sales team to do it needs a high density population to make it work.

Living in isolated rural North Yorkshire with its thinly peopled areas was not suitable for it. She was used to being her own boss with her own part time team but the only areas where such opportunities and they were few in number existed at all were related to farming and farm equipment about which she knew nothing and had no desire to explore either.

Going back to being an employee did not appeal either with the area's total lack of suitable jobs or things to do.

This deeply bored her and sent her down into a cycle of depression.

---

[12] Avon Calling http://news.sky.com/story/1660059/avon-calling-the-uk-as-cosmetics-firm-moves-hqCalling

The Army does not cater for Army wives, only soldiers.

Army wives are simply the camp followers of their partners, expected to pack up their lives at short notice when new postings come through.

For the bulk of her day television rather than Fred was her constant companion.

They stated to drift apart before they even got together properly like ships passing in the night.

He wondered what would happen when he returned to the UK at the end of his tour of duty.

That was in the future.

Helping guard the engineers restoring the water and drainage facilities along Route 601 was the immediate task in the reconstruction of Afghanistan. An area of about 500 metres wide running along each side of the route was now well served with irrigation and producing healthy crops helping to bring about a less hostile local farming population who could also see the foundations of schools and health centres starting to be built in the area as well.

Aside from his normal duties Fred had also started to think about his future outside of the Army.

Security and personal bodyguard work were both obvious possibilities, so was being a mercenary.

There was always a demand for troops hardened by recent combat experience for similar conflict situations worldwide.

Watching the engineers working on the drainage systems in Helmand had also brought back memories of his old trade in plastering working with his father who was a small general builder before he'd decided to join the Army.

He smiled to himself at the memories, Fred the Spread.

The final remaining days flew past. Suddenly, it was time to say goodbye to Helmand and his fellow squaddies at Bastion who were a closer family than he'd known in real life.

Back in the UK at Catterick there was no Chardonnay to meet him on the tarmac. She'd texted him to say she was at Bingo Bingo and couldn't make it.

Chapter 5

SuperStore Security

Fred made his decision after a period of work release at SuperStore in his final weeks in the Army. He'd looked at the mercenary possibilities that were available, the personal bodyguard opportunities and the security jobs. Many of them were part-time only and subject to demand for festival and big event work.

He weighed up the possibilities and the pros and cons of all of them.

After years of working in a top down organisation with its Strategy, Tactics and Operations pushed down from on high he was suddenly outside of his comfort zone.

It was no longer the organisation with its military priorities dovetailing into the political agenda which dictated what he could do and say.

He was used to working within a tight unit with each unit

member knowing their role. Each one knew the strength and experience of each other.

He was an Operations man responsible for making the Strategy and Tactics handed down from on high work on the ground.

The civilian world that he was moving into was totally different from what he had experienced. You were largely on your own making your own decisions.

The mercenary opportunities open to him didn't really appeal and were soon rejected by him as being in parts of the world which were too unstable.

Personal bodyguard openings soon went the same way. He had never been a solo operator, he was a team player.

That brought him to the security options. Should he simply supplement his Army pension with regular security weekend work outside football grounds. This could be topped up with seasonal big event festival work running over a few days at a time or should he stick with the pattern of an ordered existence to which he'd been accustomed.

It was the work release period with a big supermarket as a security officer which made his decision for him.

It ticked all the boxes of what he'd been used to:

He was part of a team.

He had a uniform.

He had regular hours with predictable duties.

He had the opportunity to build a new family life with Chardonnay to replace the Army family which he was shortly leaving.

He could use many of the skills which he'd acquired working in Army Operations.

The work release came to an end, he applied for the Security Manager's post and got it.

Fred was proud to wear his uniform, he was a uniform man.

As Security Manager at SuperStore, scanning the screens for hostiles and visually checking the aisles for danger and threats suited him.

It was warfare in another theatre of war.

Throughout his life as far back as he could remember, he'd always been in uniform starting with a Babygro, graduating into a sheriff's outfit when not wearing school uniform, then the Army Cadets.

Before the Army grabbed him, he had briefly worked for his father who was a general builder and quickly developed a specialism in the building team in plastering and moulding as Fred the Spread.

He was the business. He knew it, they knew it, he was simply the best in the gang.

But it was the call of uniform, the opportunity to fight non-conformity around the world, and be part of a disciplined body bringing order to where there was chaos which really motivated him finally into signing up for the Regular Army.

After a long career of fighting non-conformity his new role as Security Manager simply carried on his life's continuity.

From his raised podium at the top of the store he could

observe everything, the prowlers around the shelves loitering close to the yellow dump bins in the centre of the aisles before doing a swift switchback between the fresh meat and fish counters to the high value cosmetics.

During his work release he'd checked out the store to test its security using his Army experience, immediately identifying the weak points to bring up his interview.

The worst was the fresh veg and flowers Green Zone with no protection since nobody thought that anyone would bother pinching a carrot or a swede..

Fred wasn't sure that such a lax attitude was still in order with social attitudes changing under the Green Healthy Eating Agenda.

'Remember 5 a day[13],' he constantly reminded his Security Staff, 'Stealthy, healthy hostiles nicking a carrot slims both them and SuperStore's profits as well!'

High value small items had minimal protection.

No protection on the open fish and meat counters or those which were staffed or behind glass.

On his days off he still used to make regular reconnaissance trips into the store to test its security.

Donning his old camouflage fatigues from Helmand he hid under the multi-tiered fresh flower display in the Green Zone, watching, waiting.

Looking through the Japanese Lilies display he discovered a big security lapse.

---

[13] Five A Day http://www.nhs.uk/livewell/5aday/Pages/5ADAYhome.aspx

Suspects were weight matching bagged veg and bottles of spirit substituting spirits for veg into the empty bag then off immediately to Self Service or hiding it using the fresh rhubarb as a dead letter box to pick up later if they thought that plain clothes security had tagged them.

Weight matching was also a big problem on the beer section with suspects substituting the contents of Blue non-alcoholic Becks carton carriers with regular alcoholic Becks, a loss of £3.50 on a carton of 6 bottles.

'So simple' he thought, 'but so effective'

'You really need helicopter support for the blind spots,' he told the startled Store Manager at their regular security meetings, 'The best overhead spotter area that you've got is the upstairs restaurant but that only gives half a view.'

'As a minimum, you need those Maplin's £50 Helicopters with Cameras Bluetoothed into the security system to cover them.'

The fitness of the Security staff was another concern for Fred.

He had always kept himself fit while he was in the Army, a necessary requirement in order to pass the annual British Forces Test. The BFT ensured that Army personnel had a minimum level of fitness in order to do their job.

Fred believed that the Security staff at SuperStore simply were not fit enough to pursue shoplifters and set about bringing them up to scratch.

He cut off a small area of the Goods Inward yard to set up a course for the Security staff to practice catching thieves making off with unpaid goods.

With his fitness, he played the role of the thief making off with a box of whoopsie canned goods. His pursuer had to catch him, dodging the trollies which Fred had strategically placed or rolled into their path before he reached the end of the measured run which was equivalent to the width of the store.

Having set the timed target, they then switched roles.

Chapter 6

TWATS, SATSUMOS & FRISATS

Teamwork also greatly concerned him. It simply didn't exist in Security. The problem was that his Security staff were largely part-timers working different shifts so it was difficult to weld them into the tight coherent units with their own identity with each member knowing each other's strengths and weaknesses.

He gave each group their own identity based on the days that they worked.

The three groups were identified as TWATS (Tuesdays, Wednesdays & Thursdays), SATSUMOS (Saturdays, Sundays & Mondays) and FRISATS (Fridays & Saturdays)

He decided to adopt the Diamond formation favoured in the Army for guarding a location with a cordon, Diamond In for watching and containing what happened inside, Diamond Out for repelling any external threat trying to enter the theatre area.

The Security staff soon got used to the teamwork and positions they were required to adopt to ensure the security of the shop floor.

Then came Feedback & Performance to maintain morale and staff satisfaction.

Like the pictures of the Store Manager and the rest of the Management Team which were just inside the Store Entrance, Fred felt that Store Security personnel should also have recognition and his idea was accepted by the Management.

Every month you had a Security Staff 'Employee of the Month' displayed on the Store Picture Gallery but only in Silhouette which Fred had downloaded onto his Android tablet.

It was part of Fred's Standing Orders talk to his staff at the start of every shift.

'Openness and Secrecy, let the hostiles know that we're there but undercover and not identified.'

From his Helmand days of sweeping the way forward for mines and IEDs to minimise casualties he coined the retail shop floor mantra.

'Remember the Tesco Pink Yogurt lawsuit. Watch the floor for any innocuous material lying there. I don't want any slip and trip incidents on any watch.'[14]

With fitness, teamwork, feedback and recognition firmly established in the group, Fred felt better prepared for his task.

---

[14] Tesco Pink Yogurt Case
https://en.wikipedia.org/wiki/Ward_v_Tesco_Stores_Ltd

The first pieces of his strategy and tactics were starting to come together. He allowed himself a brief smile of satisfaction.

Chapter 7

Sid's Store Strategy

It was all coming together for Fred, even more so when Sid joined the SuperStore staff as Merchandising Manager.

It was his previous retail experience where he'd won an innovative marketing award from The Grocer, his reputation as a can do man, the problem solver, lady charmer and joker that had swung it for him.

He could schmooze the customers with his banter pushing them into buying the targeted offers.

'Too many Trans Fats, Ma'am? Then stop looking at Tumblr', he'd say.

'Oh! You are awful, hahaha,' was the usual reply.

It was Sid who saw how Fred's idea on Profiling could also help to cut down the random queues at tills, straggling outward across the shop floor which stopped the Security Staff from having a clear view across the store.

Using kettling and putting everybody in one queue with all the checkouts banked together the floor area cleared more quickly.

No more frayed tempers from having joined the wrong queue and getting stuck behind a shopper with a missing price label or only half of a BOGOF (Buy One Get One Free).

It also enabled Sid to promote local produce and push Besharat and Nick's TALIBAN TORA BORA business.

Walking along the checkout queue with trays of Afghan specialties he was able to blag the waiting shoppers.

'A Hundred Splendid Buns, Ma'am, there must be one for you,' he announced to all and sundry, watching as they eyed up the multi-coloured Abgoosht on flatbreads before making their choice.

It was followed up with mini glasses of Nick's real ales to wash them down.

He regaled the munching customers with stories of Afghanistan and dropping in Prince Harry's name in his helicopter tales.

'I've always mixed in Royal Circles,' he confided to his audience, 'my first job when I was at school was a P/T one at Burger King.'

They all laughed at the joke.

'Happy customers are spending customers,' he said to Fred.

Sid dwelled on how his early life prior to joining the regular Army had helped.

He had been an actor, classically trained in the best British tradition, three years at RADA[15] followed by three years at ALDI in the store at Stratford upon Avon, the home of Shakespearean England.

He fulfilled many supporting roles, stacking shelves, flattening the cardboard boxes into the Unitainer for

---

[15] https://www.rada.ac.uk/ Royal Academy of Dramatic Art

recycling, distributing the weekly leaflet with special offers on fishing rods, scaffolding poles, frogman suits, heavy road drills, one-off wine purchases and huge containers of milk etc. on the Stratford on Avon High St. to Sir Peter Hall and other thespians and bargain hunters etc.

It was his hard work in ALDI putting in the graft which gave him his first principal starring role as an actor.

In order to boost trade at the branch he had donned the full frogman outfit, complete with googles and flippers, sprayed himself with the water hose outside for the garden plants and flowers. Dripping, he flip flopped his way to the refrigerated section.

With a dramatic jump he landed on top of the Offer of the Week, the fresh whole salmon, grabbed the largest one and turned to the customers in the aisle, shouting triumphantly,

'I've got it, I've finally got it!! I lost it in the English Channel for a while, but finally tracked it up the Avon!! Quick, quick, you'd best buy these others before more frogmen arrive to grab them!!'

The astonished shoppers momentarily froze, then quickly recovered and made a mad dash for the fridges to quickly empty them of the salmon at bargain prices.

It made the front page of the local rag.

FROGMAN NETS FISH BARGAIN IN ALDI

It also won him a Retail Trade award for innovative comedy marketing in The Grocer trade magazine.

It was after this when his big break didn't materialise that made his mind up, well actually it wasn't, his German bosses didn't get his innovative marketing and showed him the door.

He joined the Regular Army.

It was something that had always been at the back of his mind from watching *It Ain't Half Hot, Mum*[16]on television when he was a kid. He was always a joker, the classroom entertainer and he now had an acting training giving him the professional skills in delivery and presence.

Many well-known names in British Theatre and Comedy had made it big through association with Combined Services Entertainments (CSE). He listed them off, Kenneth Williams, Spike Milligan, Harry Secombe, Des O'Connor, Frank Carson, the list just went on and on.

He was telling all this to the Army Careers Officer (ACO) when he signed up at an Army Exhibition at the Lower Pennines Jobcentre and his expectations of being of great value to the CSE.

The ACO agreed and assured him that personal preferences were always taken into account, that humour was an absolute essential in an Army environment and the often stressful situations that troops found themselves in and days later Sid was at Catterick on his basic training.

The Army was true to the ACO's assurances and showed its inherent sense of humour. He became a gunner and started his Army career in Northern Ireland,moving through various dangerous postings in his Army service which ended at Camp Bastion in Afghanistan.

His presentation skills and sense of fun soon attracted the

---

[16] BBC TV Comedy Show
http://www.nhs.uk/livewell/5aday/Pages/5ADAYhome.aspx

attention of CSE and he frequently joined the entertainers on their tours of Army bases.

He remembered his first appearance at a joint British and US Army Concert at Bastion with a load of perfectly tanned blonde US female GIs in the front rows who he had been eyeing up from behind the curtains.

Introduced by the MC as Gunner Sid from the Lower Pennines he limped on to the stage clutching his crotch and grabbed the offered mike.

'I'm just out of hospital after my vasectomy,' he said to some nervous laughs from the audience.

Then straightening up he announced, 'Now, I'll be firing blanks all over Yanks.'

It brought the house down. It was that first appearance which rubberstamped his reputation as both a ladies' man and funny guy.

Chapter 8

The Night Manager

Royston the Night Manager sat back in his chair and smiled to himself looking at a picture of his fiancée on his desk.

It was a good clear one showing her perfect figure and tan in the Atlantic sunshine, taken when they'd holidayed in Costa Teguise, Lanzarote.

Long lazy days on the loungers around the pool at Club Lanzarote, followed by an evening stroll down to the Teguise

Waterfront bars. Hennessey's [17] quickly became their favourite with its affable Dublin landlord Richard Devine.

It was chatting to Richard who had lived in Lanzarote for years on where the perfect spot in Teguise for popping the question was that made up his mind.

It was at the Villa Toledo[18] restaurant just hanging off the edge of the cliff overlooking the Atlantic, a perfect location, over a perfect dinner with perfect timing to make them a perfect couple.

He'd arranged all of it through Richard with the Front of House man.

She'd instantly accepted and at Royston's signal to him, the staff immediately surrounded them with ringing bells, flash photography and champagne for everyone on the patio to celebrate the occasion.

Then it was back to England to the night shifts and a marathon of scouting out suitable available venues, endless tours of bridal wear shops and fittings, the arguments over the best man and bridesmaids.

 Then there was the hard bit of compiling guest lists, who to leave in, who to throw out, who was coming to the reception, who was only being invited to the evening doo.

Finally, finally for everyone's nerves it was now coming to a conclusion.

---

[17] Hennesseys https://www.tripadvisor.co.uk/ShowUserReviews-g659633-d1952949-r123788234-Hennessey_s-Costa_Teguise_Lanzarote_Canary_Islands.html
[18] Villa Toledo https://www.tripadvisor.co.uk/Restaurant_Review-g659633-d1463069-Reviews-Villa_Toledo_Restaurant-Costa_Teguise_Lanzarote_Canary_Islands.html

'Only two more weeks,' he thought, 'then it's off to the seaside for the Stag Doo.'

He'd been off happy pills for months but had to call into the surgery for another prescription.

'Weddings and marriage, always stressful,' said the sympathetic GP.

'Oh No,' said Royston, 'It's not the wedding. It's the new Security Manager, a nutter driving us all bonkers.'

'Ex-Army but still sees himself as Army. A nightmare. He's got Floor Security stationed around in Diamond formation. That's how the Army stakes out a position. They take up a Diamond In formation firing into the killing zone without any possibility of mishits, Blue on Blue, or firing out, Diamond Out to thwart an attack into the zone from outside, it gives 360 degrees cover. He's got these flaming helicopters flying around, hovering, and then shooting away to another section.'

'He's also started Profiling and put all the Curry Ranges, Tofu and Organic produce together.'

'Why?' I said to him, 'it's driving both customers and stackers bonkers. They don't know where anything is any more and we work twice as hard restocking.'

'Profiling,' he said, 'To channel Johnny Foreigner, hostiles and fellow travellers/sympathisers into the killing zone where Diamond can keep a really close eye on them.'

'Fellow travellers/sympathisers?,' I said.

'Guardian readers,' he said, 'they're all into that Tofu, Quinoa and Organic stuff and although they might see shoplifting, they'd never tell you.'

Big corporates bring it on themselves their conscience would tell them.

'Last week, I saw a hostile push past a Guardian reader with a big box of Our Finest. Not a word.'

'For the Foodbank,' the hostile muttered, running for the door.

'Diamond Out pulled him down in Disabled Parking.'

Royston recalled the good old days before Fred arrived. You came in with the Packers, worked your balls off for a couple of hours, brewed up, tucked into whoopsie sandwiches and going out of date cakes, then free until about 6.00am when the dairy produce and morning goods started to arrive along with the newspapers and magazines.

His other job had been to move the unsold editions down to the Goods Bay for collection.

That was his brainwave light bulb moment.

With multiple identities he'd stacked up thousands of points in the Rewards Club from the Mail and Money off coupons from magazines.

It financed his Stag Doo.

Four £15 per night chalets in North Yorkshire booked with Mail Rewards and a big saving due on booze and food they were taking when he cashed in the remaining Reward Points for SuperStore Gift Cards. On his Membercard Points account they'd get the full 20p a litre off the fuel as well.

Darren, his best man, had managed to borrow two Sunshine

Variety Club Minibuses and got a great deal from ALDI on wetsuits they'd need for the cliff jumping

'Life was good, even better in a couple of weeks,' he chuckled, 'Time for a fag.'

He set off to the old Staff Room which had no smoke alarm.

It was locked.

'Strange,' he thought, 'But, never mind.'

He exited the Fire Door and looked around for a dodgy sun lounger to block it while outside.

'Strange,' he thought, 'The cleaners must have shifted them.'

Finding a piece of shelving he pushed it through the outside handles to keep it shut.

Lighting up, he blew a very contented smoke ring into the night sky.

'Fire doesn't knock,' said a voice beside him, as he jumped, startled.

It was Fred, always on duty.

Chapter 9

BASSTARDS

Fred always had doubts about Royston. Not only Royston but also his friend Darren, a frequent visitor to see the Night Manager.

'Not one of us, either of them,' he'd confided to Diamond,

'Keep your eyes on them, possible sleepers or lilywhites for the SuperStore opposition.'

He had joined the staff association, BASSTARDS, the British Association of Store Security Trade & Retail Distribution Staff and always browsed their newsletter for the latest trends in security.

He'd also started to contribute tips to tighten up store security and was getting favourable feedback on the closed Facebook website for his helicopter and other teambuilding ideas like Diamond, Security Employee of the Month and staff fitness.

He liked closed Facebook Groups like BASSTARDS where you could discuss matters with your peers to see if there was any mileage in them.

Sometimes, what seems like a barmpot idea to outsiders, when put forward by practitioners like himself suddenly makes perfect sense.

That was the case with his helicopter idea, it was simply a case of transferring an idea which worked into a different sphere.

That fitted in with his Army experience in Operations, you could post anything, from blue sky thinking, to suggesting a well tried method and get worldwide response and feedback.

It was like having your own Consumer Panel, Peer Group or Star Chamber to bounce ideas off, get suggestions from feedback, modify, refocus or drop your suggestion if it was generally considered to be a no-goer. He was a regular poster on Facebook for its more or less instant response.

He had tried out his store helicopter idea on it.

Bert MI6 -A Chopper!! Defo! Every store security manager should have a chopper!!

MontySAS –That probably rules out female security managers Bert MI6!

BertMI6 –LOLOLOL!! Top 1, MontySAS. Laffing my balls off!!

Fred2014 - @ MontySAS @BertMI6 best Unfriend Harriet Harman before she sees this exchange, ROFL!!

Fred's suspicions about Darren increased when he spotted him one day wearing a 38 Degrees Save Our Forests T-Shirt with a hanging Social Worker type Photo Name Badge around his neck carrying an Ocado bag for life.

Home shopping and delivery to the door were both anathema to Fred. He'd identified web shopping with home delivery as a major threat to the future of SuperStore and the Store Security industry and had posted his thoughts about it on BASSTARDS Facebook page on breaking the stay at home shopping secret coded messages.

GDA! BBW B&M BOGOF on soaps, HTH[19]
Good Deal Alert! Bath & Body Works Brick and Mortar store has Buy One Get One Free on soaps, Hope This Helps!

It was Bert MI6 with his black ops experience who started to solve the problem with fake online vouchers which wouldn't print.

He followed it up with short time dated discount coupons for beers which once activated had to be used within 10 minutes. The streets outside the store often featured out of

---

[19] Article Source: http://EzineArticles.com/40340

breath fat blokes with pelmet T shirts hanging over their beer bellies running towards SuperStore with laptop in hand trying to get there before the coupon ran out.

More often than not, they didn't make it, but sitting on top of a stack of Stella Artois in the aisle, sweating and panting, often decided they needed even more to make up for their efforts.

'Two strikes against him,' Fred thought, putting Darren into his miscellaneous category of possible fellow traveller/sympathisers, undercover agents and web shoppers.

He moved the helicopter into position to follow as Darren moved around the aisles to see if he merited a full BASSTARDS scrutiny check.

'Yes, yes, yes!,' he inwardly shouted.

His sixth sense had proved correct again as Darren picked up a Guardian and hit the third strike for blacklisting. Quickly zapping a couple of mug shots of Darren, he saved them to do a comparison Skipease search on Google Images.

Fred had taken over the old downstairs staff room as a back-up Security Command & Control Centre and wired it into the main system.

'Remember Nairobi![20],' he said to Diamond who all thoroughly approved of his forward planning.

'If we get al-Shabaab in here, we simply retreat downstairs and run the Ops from there.'

---

[20] Westgate Terror Attack
https://en.wikipedia.org/wiki/Westgate_shopping_mall_attack

He'd set up the returned sun loungers with dodgy springs as a Field Hospital and used to retreat down here on his breaks to read and comment online on the BASSTARDS newsletter and Facebook page. Browsing the papers while the laptop was firing up, it was tabloid Summer Promotion time again in the tabloids, preceded by ££££s in the strapline.

The headlines always screamed the promotion to you.

Mr. Moneybags is BACK!!! for the British Seaside Summer Season screamed the Sun. If you spot Mr. Moneybags all you have to do is wave your copy of the Sun, shout 'You're Mr. Moneybags and I claim my £20 and the dosh is yours, all in your super, soaraway Sun this Summer.'

The laptop was ready and he downloaded Darren's photographs into Skipease and waited for the comparison search on Google Images to show up.

It took about 30 seconds to appear. He was so shocked that he slipped off his chair onto a field hospital bed getting a dodgy spring lodged in his trousers.

'I knew it! I knew it! I knew it!,' he kept repeating.

There was Darren on the screen boasting about his successful attack as an urban guerrilla on a big corporate SuperStore. Not just any SuperStore but the very same SuperStore where Fred was now sat transfixed by the image and words he was seeing and hearing on the screen.

Troubled by what he had just seen and heard, Fred closed down the laptop and went upstairs pondering what to do with his discovery.

Chapter 10

The Mid Day Post

The post had arrived.

Julie the Office Administrator dropped a big registered post envelope on Fred's podium.

'You must have won the lottery, Fred,' she said, 'it's probably stuffed with money.'

She laughed and walked away. He turned the envelope over, and then the logo caught his eye. It was from BASSTARDS. Curious, he pulled it open.

Inside was a handwritten note, a typed letter, a map and a large embossed Invitation. He quickly scanned the typed letter.

It started with Congratulations then went on to say that he had been nominated by the Executive Committee to receive their highest accolade, the Prophet Award for services to Store Security with directions and accommodation voucher for the National Conference in two weeks.

Both excited and stunned he then read the handwritten note.

It was from BertMI6.

'Congratulations, Fred,' it said, 'Very few members receive the Prophet Award and this is the first occasion that I can remember someone in their first 12 months of membership ever going straight to the very top. Normally they staircase the grades but you've gone straight to the very top with your forward, visionary thinking. See you at Conference.'

Fred was dazed.

The two shocks in a very short time of seeing Darren as an urban warrior, then the Prophet Award, left him slightly giddy and he gripped the podium to keep his balance.

It was Darren and a friend, almost certainly Royston, who'd become a YouTube sensation at the time of the horsemeat burger scandal.

Darren and friend had dressed up in a pantomime horse outfit, trotted into the store unchallenged and made straight for the chilled meat open fridges.

'Daaad, Maaam,Brooother,' they'd shouted into the burger display as they trotted past, 'I'll never see you again. How could they? No more days out galloping together in the meadows. How could they? How could they? Oh my God, murderers, barbarians!!'

It became a YouTube massive copied and shared everywhere, unleashing a flood of horse burger jokes.

It was a store security disaster.

He decided to see Stuart the Store Manager right away.

Stuart watched the video and smiled, he'd seen it several times, both with HQ and others. Although it affected his store he had to laugh at the ingenuity of the prank.

He looked at the chopper zapped images of Darren and compared them to the YouTube Video.

There was a certain likeness, he had to concede.

'And the second one in the pantomime horse is, I believe to be Royston,' said Fred.

Stuart immediately fastened on to Fred's assertion but managed to hide his excitement.

He knew Fred was 100% wrong.

Stuart bit into his burger as Fred then told him about the BASSTARDS nomination.

Fred reckoned that Stuart didn't really appreciate all the new ideas and successes that he'd made on the Security front.

Stuart was aware that shoplifting was way, way down on comparable stores and had attracted HQ attention. Every week HQ geeks were in store to study Fred's methods for possible cascading around the others.

On the other hand he had more staff on the sick than other branches as well with the constant close surveillance of Fred and Diamond. He himself was working almost every weekend to provide cover and he was on rota to work the forthcoming Bank Holiday weekend.

The Conference where Fred was to receive his Prophet Award was over the same four day busy Bank Holiday weekend

Stuart knew what his answer to Fred would be but hid his intention well and sucked in his cheeks as if considering the matter. Looking at Fred with a frown he thumbed through the Store Manager's Staff Guide pretending to look for something.

'Ah!'he finally said, 'I knew there was some wriggle room somewhere.'

He showed Fred Section 2.3, 'Local management has discretion to grant up to 4 days discretionary paid leave to staff who have made an outstanding contribution to the Company at local store level', it read.

Turning to Fred he said, 'And there's absolutely no question that you certainly fulfil that requirement. I'm giving you 4 days paid leave to cover the entire Conference, to network, spread the word and hopefully bring back even more ideas. Well done!'

Fred was quite stunned.

He had badly misjudged Stuart. He'd previously felt that Stuart thought he was a nuisance and didn't rate him at all and had confided his misgivings to Diamond.

'Not really one of us either', he'd said.

He suddenly realised that Stuart appreciated that he was doing an excellent job and he'd been wholly mistaken.

He stood up, saluted Stuart, thanked him and marched out the office door.

When he'd gone, Stuart swallowed the last of his burger, allowed himself a big smile, settled back, giving a loud horse laugh , "Wheeeeeeeeeeeeeeeaah!" which echoed down the corridor.

Suddenly, working the Bank Holiday weekend was a great idea,

'Four days, four days without Fred around,' he thought, 'It's even better than being on holiday!!'

He got up, walked to the end of the office, looked at his desk wondering if he could still do it in such short a space.

He hadn't been in training for several weeks.

He ran up the floor, jumped, lifting his feet clear, sailed over the desk and landed safely on the other side.

'Wheeeeeeeeeeeeeeeaah!' he horse laughed again.

He hadn't noticed Julie the Office Administrator.

She saw Stuart finish the burger, walk to the far wall, run, then jump over his desk with a great 'Wheeeeeeeeeeeeeeeaah!'

'You alright Stu?,' she enquired.

'Never felt better, Jools,' he said.

Standing beside her he pawed the floor, horse style , slapped himself a few times on the backside and with a final 'Wheeeeeeeeeeeeeeeaah!,' galloped past her onto the shop floor.

Chapter 11

The Stag Doo

Royston woke up in bed with a bad head and a very dried out mouth, easily done in the company of friends, too much booze and song.

What's a celebration without all these factors being present?

The Stag Group had arrived at the chalets the previous evening and indulged a bit too freely, too early and the loud music was still pounding in his head.

He wished he was fitter for the weekend's activities that Darren had planned. He used to run a lot to keep fit before Fred arrived, sometimes alone or other times with Stuart, the

Store Manager.

Royston and Stuart were both fell runners in training for the Northern Premier, the leading and toughest run in the North. The last time that they'd run out together was on their joint day off weeks ago with a tough practice, hurdling and jumping the rocks and crags down the fells of the Lower Pennines outside the town.

It was the same day that the pantomime horse fiasco and video happened. The next day Darren came in to see both Royston and Stuart to apologise for all the trouble and publicity that the horsemeat video had caused them.

Darren was a fellow runner on marathons. He was a Social & Community Worker with Adult Services with a strong social conscience, active in protests against cutbacks but feeling that making impossible budgets work for his clients was much better than simply trying to oppose change and different practices being foisted on him from above.

Clients were always his first priority. His twin brother David was an anarchist and thought differently. It was David and a fellow Occupy London activist in costume who had staged the pantomime horse stunt at Stuart's store.

After breakfast Darren rounded them all up, black wetsuits on, into the minibuses. The Iron Man Weekend, planned with Stags R Us was a tough one.

Cliff jumping into the North Sea, a swim around the resort head to the island, a Roast Hog Barbecue and overnight camp, then a 10 mile bike ride back over the causeway when the tide was out.

The loud *oi!Hoi!oi!Hoi!, I'm the man, oi!Hoi!oi!Hoi!, I'm the man* music with heavy drum and bass beat pumped them up for the challenge.

Both minibuses roared into the Conference Centre Car Park, the doors opened and the *oi! Hoi!oi!Hoi!* music flooded over the sea front. Royston was the first out of the minibus, shouting, 'Last one in the sea is a ponce!!'

He ran towards the Centre leading the chanting, 'We're all going to jump in the sea!!'

The others responded, 'Last one in, it won't be me.' challenging each other to a faster pace. Jumping over the sand drifts and rocks they passed the side of the Centre heading for the narrow path to the cliff head.

The Scottish Power man on his ladder working on the Centre power supply fuse box jumped out of the way.

'Bloody hell!,' he said to himself, 'bloody hell, barmpots!! This town's gone bloody bonkers!!'

Jostling and elbowing each other, competitive, sweating and panting, they made for the top, jumping into the North Sea with a loud 'Gerrrrrooonnnimmmo!!' on their way down and started to swim around the head towards the town centre and the island in the bay.

Chapter 12

The BASSTARDS Conference

BASSTARDS was created almost entirely by BertMI6 when he left Army Special Ops. Like Fred he had been made redundant in the Defence Cuts Review.

The Army, particularly Special Ops, had taken up the biggest chunk of his adult life.

He'd scouted out the usual possible avenues available to him in civilian life where he could possibly make a mark and earn a nice little number as well.

Mercenary work, though readily available did not appeal to him, he was a military man, in it because he believed in it and not simply for the money. His days of engaging in gun battles on distant shores were also well behind him.

Similarly, personal security and bodyguard work did not appeal either.

He was an organiser, the man with the grand plan, the strategy, the man who built things from the ground up who put all the pieces together and made them work and needed a suitable outlet for the experience in team building which he'd acquired over the years in the Army.

He finally found the niche that he was looking for in the Security Industry which was virgin territory in the United Kingdom badly organised, patchy and fragmented.

It was an opportunity which presented itself where he could use his acquired skills to build something from the ground up which could provide a model of excellence and good practice and be a leader in its' field.

The Government had recognised that the whole Security Industry need to be sorted out. Store Security like Door Security was a disorganised mess. The need to train, accredit and regulate became Government initiatives and the Security Industry Authority (SIA) was formed to bring order to the industry and begin the accreditation of security staff and weed out those who were unsuitable.

BASSTARDS was one of the first accredited SIA bodies and specialised in store security.

It had three levels of awards Prophets, Apostles and Followers.

Prophets were visionaries of where store security could go in the future with 'blue sky thinking.'

Apostles took the Prophets' vision and spread it far and wide.

Followers faithfully put in action the Apostles' instructions.

BASSTARDS was a small group.

'We all know who our biggest enemies are,' he said introducing Fred to Conference, almost spitting out the word, 'Mercenaries!! The lowest form of life in store security, only in it for the money, with no training, no real interest or pride in the job.'

Conference applauded .

'But with our newest Prophet, WE START THE FIGHTBACK!!'

Fred stepped forward, exchanged salutes, then spread both arms out as if carrying a heavy weight in each hand.

He asked Conference, 'If Moses was a Store Security Manager today would he still write his instructions on tablets of stone?'

'No, no ,no!!,'he said and with a flourish held up an Android tablet.

'Today's Moses would have put them on an Android, HDMIed output to a big screen with an App for Download in the Google Store so that everyone on the mountain could see them!'

'But too many stores are STILL in the stone tablet age.. WE WILL CHANGE THAT and kick out the mercenaries!'

He paused. Through the Conference Centre windows he saw two minibuses speeding into the car park.

Doors opened, with loud thump, thump, music and a large group of young men all dressed in black wetsuits jumped out, running towards the Centre chanting.

Startled, he snatched the tablet, tapped the Binocular App and focused on the group.

The leader was Royston, closely followed by Darren, Royston chanted something, the rest responded, he watched the determined faces with horror, the gritted teeth, the determination, the jostling and elbowing, all trying to get there first. He'd pictured that scene before in Army service, the look of fanatics determined to kill him.

'Barricade the doors, we're being attacked!,' he shouted, running for the stairs. Too late, the lights went out, plunging the Centre into darkness.

Feeling his way downstairs in pitch blackness, to the ground floor, heart pounding there was an eerie silence.

Suddenly, the lights came back up. The foyer was totally empty.

Puzzled, frightened, he went to the main door, followed by some other BASSTARDS, curious at his behaviour and the turn of events.

'Where were his attackers? Where had they gone?' he thought, looking back at the Car Park then the cliff path just in time to see the last black wetsuit jump over the cliff.

He ran up the path to see all of them swimming furiously towards the headland and the town centre.

He suddenly realised that the power knock out had been a decoy, a false flag, to knock him off his guard and he panicked.

Their real target suddenly dawned on him.

It was the brand new SuperStore in the town centre and they were making strong progress in the water towards it.

Nobody had ever considered an attack from the sea before.

He turned and tried to run back down the path to warn SuperStore Security.

Chapter 13

Meltdown

His way back down the cliff was blocked.

Attracted by the loud thumping *oi!Hoi!oi!Hoi…I'm the man* music and the Stags running and jostling their way up to the cliff top, a large group of burly blokes wearing Lonsdale T-shirts and beer bellies were panting up the path towards him waving copies of The Sun and shouting at him.

'You're Mr. Moneybags and I claim my £20!'

He was being edged closer and closer to the cliff edge.

A fuse blew in his head. The internal screen in his brain faded into blackness and the message NO LIVE OUTPUT scrolled up it, the cached pages of previous memories started to roll, the baying mob, the sand and rocks, the hot sun, the threatening group of young men in black wetsuits suddenly morphed into the black robes of the Taliban.

Physically, he was on a cliff in North Yorkshire. Mentally, he was back in Helmand.

He sank to the ground, shaking uncontrollably, gibbering and curled himself up in the foetal position.

The NHS Ambulance crew struggled through the crowd, strapped Fred to the stretcher and started their way back down.

Back at the chalets Bob, Bill, Doris and Frieda sat in the morning sunshine unaware of the drama happening around the Conference Centre.

They were all long term Volunteers at Darren's Community Centre. A few stags had dropped out leaving a spare empty chalet.

They liked Darren, he valued them and told them so frequently. With the budget cuts he needed them more than ever to keep all the activities going.

In this new era of austerity, volunteers were no longer an extra on top of permanent staff, they were the permanent staff and he made sure that their contribution was always rewarded and recognised.

It was he who suggested that they come for the weekend to

the spare accommodation and squared it with Royston.

They were delighted. It was their first seaside holiday together in 25 years.

All four had first met together when Bob and Bill had finished their stint in Akrotiri in Cyprus and they'd dropped off at the Fusiliers' Camp in Blackpool. It was Bill's idea to telegram Frieda to see if she and Doris would come up.

Excitedly, after finishing their shift at Sankey's Soap in Ancoats, they'd grabbed new red stilettos on Shudehill, caught the train to Blackpool North, then the Bispham tram to Starr Gate.

Bob and Bill were there waiting for them in uniform. With linked arms, chatting and laughing, they made their way through the Illuminations to the Manchester Arms, a little piece of England's greatest party City, transported to the Lancashire Coast, for Dance Craze Night.

Together they jived,[21] twisted,[22] hucklebucked[23] and locomotioned[24] the night away.

At throwing out time, Bob suggested the Tower Ballroom and in uniform, blagged them all in for the last dance. Cheek to cheek, they waltzed round the floor to Dean Martin's *Memories are made of this*[25]

The men carried both women on their shoulders back to the Winter Gardens. Their new stilettos had wrecked their feet

---

[21] https://www.youtube.com/watch?v=qOrQTh_Cq7U Johnny Otis
[22] https://www.youtube.com/watch?v=pHGXwQeUk7M Chubby Checker
[23] https://www.youtube.com/watch?v=P33V-wnfnzs Brendan Bowyer
[24] https://www.youtube.com/watch?v=eKpVQm41f8Y Little Eva
[25] https://www.youtube.com/watch?v=NS2k43NJycE Memories are made of this

with blisters.

Bob looked at Bill and together they made a run for the Amusements on the North Shore.

The women laughed and screamed, their beehived hair falling loose as the men dropped them into two swing boats and pushed, and pushed to see who could get the highest swing.

It was Bob who started it, bursting into song with Bill Haley's *Rock Around the Clock.*[26]

'One, two, three o' clock, four o'clock rock,

'Five, six, seven, eight o'clock rock,

Bill joined him,

'Nine, ten, eleven, twelve o'clock rock,

'We're gonna' rock around the clock tonight, rock around the clock tonight …"[27]

They all joined in and for one day only, they were again the young people they had once been in Blackpool, thanks to Darren and Royston.

Chapter 14

Diagnosis & Rehabilitation

Fred had only a dim memory of the events which had brought him into the Lower Pennines Mental Health Services

---

[26] https://www.youtube.com/watch?v=ZgdufzXvjqw Rock Around the Clock
[27] https://www.youtube.com/watch?v=wWgYSoShIPM Lyrics

Unit (LPMHSU), being deeply sedated, and it was some time before he was checked out by a medic.

'You have Closed Memory Syndrome,' said the medic to him.

'Fundamentally, your mind is working within a closed loop and when you are under extreme stress, your reaction is to compare what you see with what is stored in your memory.'

'It can't break out of that loop and basically says by comparing stored images, in the case of the black wet suited group, running determinedly towards you, pumped up and chanting, this must be a Taliban attack since that is the only stored image which fits all or most of these points.'

'It morphs into the stored image and the real image, what you are seeing, is not processed any further.'

'What we have to do is break into the closed loop, open it, and instil new attitudes and ways of interpreting information being received so that numerous possibilities of what it is being seen can be made.'

'Unfreezing, instil new ways and means of interpretation, and then refreeze.'

'Have you heard of Maslow's Hammer[28]?' he said to Fred.

Fred shook his head.

'Abraham Maslow the psychologist put forward a theory which said – If all that you have is a hammer, then all you can see are nails, hence Maslow's Hammer", said the medic,

---

[28]Maslow's Hammer http://www.vectorstudy.comnagement-gurus/abraham-maslow/ma

'and that's where you are at present.'

The days passed quickly as Fred responded to treatment and slowly began to take a wider view of life as facets of his pre-Army life and Regular Army service were explored and discovered and it was building on these latent skills that his treatment concentrated on.

The treatment was to steer Fred away from his paranoia of being a target engrained during his Army days and always seeing hostiles, to turn negatives into positives.

Gradually, his obsessions with security and seeing hostiles everywhere started to fade into the background as latent skills and interests were discovered and linked together.

No longer did he feel apprehensive or expecting danger when he strolled through the sculpture park in the MHSU gardens.

The need to continually check behind each standing sculptured sheet of limestone for would be attackers or improvised devices began to fade and he started to enjoy the hidden areas of his surroundings.

He had learned to relax.

Before joining the regular Army Fred had worked with his father who was a builder where he quickly developed a specialism in plastering and moulding and acquired a working knowledge of a wide range of other trade skills as well and also a nickname, Fred the Spread.

It was these skills which had been dormant for so many years together with the leadership and group collective culture from his Army experience which had been worked on in his psychological sessions in order to weld them both together.

Chapter 15

Exit Interview

'We're sending you out on a work placement at the PASTELLS Centre (Passing on Skilled Trade Experience Lifelong Learning Services) initially as a volunteer which hopefully may develop into full-time employment,' said the psychologist to Fred as they sat facing each other over his desk.

'I'm just waiting for the PASTELLS Manager to arrive, to introduce you to each other and work out a suitable programme which satisfies both your needs and theirs.'

The buzzer on his intercom beeped.

'The PASTELLS Manager has just arrived in Reception,' announced a female voice.

'OK, Thanks just send him through,' said the psychologist rising from behind his desk and going to the office door.

Fred turned slightly in his chair as the new arrival came through the door.

Dressed in a smart suit and tie with hand outstretched with a well-trimmed head and beard, his face looked slightly familiar to Fred.

His memory banks churned around searching for a match in stored images for the person stood beside him and found one.

It was Darren.

Together they talked about what PASTELLS could do for Fred.

Darren's Community Centre had been changed with a successful Single Regeneration Budget Bid into a full Multi-Purpose Community with an Arts & Crafts Centre added on to it for Training and Reskilling.

Fred's previous Building Trade experience coupled with his Army experience was of great interest to Darren.

The mixture of trade skills and the disciplined approach which Fred had been exposed to in the Army boded well for Fred's employment prospects.

'One of our problems here is attracting the right calibre of trades people,' explained Darren, 'there is often a disjoint between those who have trade skills and their ability to pass these skills on or in fact to control a group of trainees. Both are important in order for us to succeed in our role.'

'Frequently, we come across excellent skilled tradesmen who, however, because they have worked a lifetime alone as single individuals, often lack the man management skills to stand in front of a group, impose discipline, and get them working together in a common purpose.'

'That's why your Army experience will come in useful since you have been exposed to these skills of supervising groups in a disciplined environment allied to your previous trades experience sounds exactly like the kind of individual we are looking out for.'

PASTELLS was always in need of skilled former tradesmen both as volunteers and then, if funds were available to take up part or full time employment.

'Essentially,' said Darren, 'I see the Centre developing into a broad based skills Centre widening the skills available within the community which have been lost or fallen into disuse and hopefully adding to self-employment opportunities for participants.'

'There are a number of opportunities available both in training full time participants in trades as well as providing Taster or Short Courses for DIYers who feel confident about doing work themselves. We provide them with the finishing touches that add professionalism to their efforts.'

Walking around the Centre with Darren, Fred was impressed by what he saw.

Set into the Pennines slopes its floor to ceiling glass walls gave a full view over the landscape, the ribbon development of the past and its twinkling street lamps all pushing down, the view through the elevated M62 motorway bridge, down, down, down into the sea of light at the bottom of the valley that was Cottonopolis - the city of Manchester and beyond it, the river Mersey with the Ship Canal beside it heading for Liverpool.

You had the full view of an industrial landscape being regenerated stretching in a wide vista from the West Yorkshire border to Bolton and beyond. Behind it, the wind turbines on Scout Moor slowly turned.

'This area was the Silicon Valley of the 19th century, bursting with skills and ideas from small home workshops, growing up into mills and engineering works, and exporting their products worldwide through the Port of Manchester,' said Darren.

'PASTELLS' mission is to reskill the area once more, to recreate the small workshops and make the Pennines hum with activity once again.'

He pointed out to Fred the dark mass of what had once been the largest mill in the world, now largely in darkness except for the small workshops on ground floor spreading up to the floor above.

'The renaissance and regeneration is already well underway.'

From the Pennine Sculptures in front of the PASTELLS entrance, the route led into the foyer with the Arts and Innovation Exhibition area and following along into the various training areas for bricklaying, plastering , wallpapering with electrical, electronic and carpentry and joinery areas.

The catering and food preparation areas and training restaurant, the Hive where the IT, 3D Printing and Prototype Lab were based, everywhere you looked buzzed with productive activity.

His interest in making things happen had been reawakened by Darrren's obvious infectious enthusiasm in the PASTELLS project.

He knew he could make a difference and it was agreed that he would start initially as a volunteer instructor on the Part Time Skills Courses so that both of them could see how it went.

Satisfied with the outcome Fred returned to check out of the MHSU. Its job had been done.

He shook hands with the psychologist who had been his

main caseworker and worked his way around the unit seeking out those with whom he had contact to thank them.

An old life was closing, a new beginning beckoned to him.

Chapter 16

PASTELLS

His new role as a volunteer at PASTELLS quickly developed into employment.

Fred the Spread always took the holistic view of life.

His role as a Lifelong Learning Tutor teaching the Part-time DIY Skills Course gave him the platform to spread his philosophy.

Plastering had been his trade before he joined the regular Army and his entrée into smoothing out all the highs and lows of life.

'We are all connected,' he said to his group of trainees on the New Opportunities Jobsearch Scheme, 'though sometimes we can't see it. Remember S.P.I.C.E. (turning to write it on the whiteboard) Spread Plaster In Crevices Everywhere.

He had an opinion on everything and where everything could fit in.

Pebble dashing had been his specialty before it had gone out of vogue but not before it had fashioned his view of life.

It was watching the multi-coloured pebbles and chippings being fired from the Tyrolean Projector into the soft newly rendered bed of mortar that made him realise,

As he said,

'Something switched on a lightbulb in my head, and I thought, yes, we're all in it together. Granite, flint, sandstone and limestone chippings – we've all got our own space but we're all joined in a shared space. That's what makes sense of everything, now am I right, or am I right?'

It was his mental breakdown together with his rehabilitation in the Lower Pennines MHSU which had set him on the path to spreading his philosophy further.

His voluntary work placement at PASTELLS Centre had morphed into full employment

His Disability Assessment had classed him as fit for light duties and his Personal Job Centre advisor fixed him up with a permanent PASTELLS post.

It was here that he passed his PTLLS[29] (Preparing to Teach in the Lifelong Learning Sector) and learned the acronyms and learning theories of his new calling.

Equipped with Maslow's Hierarchy[30],his Hammer and his Conscious Incompetence Ladder[31] as well, his tools for his new trade were now in his head and no longer in the back of his white van.

---

[29] PTLLS http://www.cityandguilds.com/qualifications-and-apprenticeships/learning/teaching/6302-preparing-to-teach-in-the-lifelong-learning-sector-ptlls#tab=information

[30] Maslow's Hierarchyhttp://www.simplypsychology.org/maslow.html
[31] Maslow's Conscious Incompetence Ladder.
http://www.mindtools.com/pages/article/newISS_96.htm

Like all tradesmen, although he'd been a Plasterer, specialising in pebble dashing, he had a good basic knowledge of all the other building trades as well.

In PASTELLS he quickly became indispensable, often helping out on mending plugs, putting in spur circuits, making frames for exhibits etc., as well as his own trade of plastering.

Daphne, who taught Art, Sculpture Made Easy and Cooking for One frequently called on his assistance.

Women hadn't featured much in Fred's life much since Chardonnay had done a runner with the Bingo Bingo Caller after she won the UK Weekly Jackpot.

They'd both done a bunk with her Jackpot and the night's takings to Magaluf.

She sent him a card of their new place which looked a bit like a 50 floor multistorey car park with windows and balconies, with both a ground floor and roof top bar.

It was Daphne who stirred anew his interest in women … and he couldn't help but compare her favourably against Chardonnay his wife.

Daphne could talk about Art, Sculpture, Cooking, Lateral thinking, the Green Recycling Agenda and a whole host of other interests.

Fred lapped it up like a sponge.

She also read the Guardian.

Chardonnay had rarely talked about much to him at Catterick.

Her interests were largely Primark, Bingo, Jeremy Kyle, The X Factor and Britain's Got Talent.

Seasonally it was I'm a Celebrity and the Big Brother House.

She'd once tried to be a contestant on Who Wants to Be a Millionaire but her text speak spelling had let her down and she got rejected.

As a result though, she got a lot of job offers for milliner machinist work in the local hat making factories which came in useful for her regular Jobsearch interviews.

She smoked a lot as well.

Her cooking skills were limited to putting whoopsies from Tesco in the microwave.

She read OK and Hello magazines.

Daphne opened up a whole new world for Fred.

In fairness, they hadn't got off on the right foot.

Daphne had noted Fred's multi DIY skills and sought his help in mounting her History of Art display. He was pleased to do it that very weekend.

Unfortunately she hadn't left clear instructions.

Fred had framed and wrongly mounted her Picasso print in the Caveman Art space on her wall.

It was soon changed to a new location which fitted its period in the history of art with profuse apologies from Fred to Daphne.

Chapter 17

Daphne Moves In

It was then that she decided to make Fred her project.

His years of plastering and Army service with its yearly British Forces Test (for fitness, running with a full backpack and carrying a rifle over a measured timed course, had kept his body well-toned.

She firmly gripped both his arms.

Remarking on his firm biceps she steered him around her display explaining what each section and picture meant.

'Wouldn't you simply die to pose for Degas?' she said, looking at his Woman in the Bath print, brushing against him, he thought suggestively.

Fred's indispensability and multi skills around PASTELLS rapidly brought him to the attention of the Management Committee who used him as their new poster boy for Lifelong Learning.

He glowed in the poster with his picture and Maslow's Hammer quote as a speech bubble saying,

'If all you have is a hammer, everything looks like a nail' - PASTELLS.

When a new Management post for Greening the Outdoor came up Fred applied for it and got it.

He had changed his overalls for a management white cotton coat. In Wetherspoon's he told his friends about the interview and his ideas.

'Guerilla Gardening? Just plant out every overgrown Council concrete container with flower seeds or green vegetables for the people to pick, win their hearts and minds.'

'The Conscious Incompetence Ladder? It's like Donald Rumsfeld, the US Secretary of State, once said upside down –Things we know, we know, things we know, we don't know and things we don't know , we don't know.'

'What's the one single thing that you'd want the Council to change if you got the job?' asked the Developing the Pennines Economy Officer (DTPECO) to Fred.

'Free telephone calls for the elderly,' said Fred, 'De Bono did that in Australia. He got the phone company to give free calls but limited them by putting a big lump of lead in the receiver so they wouldn't talk for too long, far too tiring to hold the receiver and no shelf in the booth to rest your arm on.'

'You could do the same here but make all of the receiver in lead, get them manufactured at the Pennine Foundry that's under threat of closure so you kill two birds with one stone, free telephone calls and saving jobs.'

The DTPECO's eyes gleamed, 'A BOGOF, buy one get one free,' he thought.

Sat in the lounge bar of the Edwin Waugh[32] with a table of foaming Spitfire and his audience hanging on to his every word, Fred felt a bit like Socrates with his group in his villa drinking wine and setting the world to rights with things that needed to be changed.

---

[32] The local Wetherspoons pub in Heywood

The more the beer flowed, the more the ideas flowed.

He pondered if Socrates had got pissed as well when the wine flowed in his villa.

He could mentally picture Socrates and his group of disciples sitting around a table in his villa philosophising and coming up with the idea of Democracy and getting so excited about it that they all burst spontaneously into song to the tune of Ken Dodd's *'Happiness.'*[33]

'Democracy, Democracy,

Me for you and you for me,

I thank Apollo that we possess,

Much more than our share of Democracy'.

He could picture Socrates and his student Plato with a glass of wine in hand standing next to him looking out of the villa window at Xenophon ploughing the field outside.

'Hey Soc!' said Plato, 'Shouldn't we tell Xen about how well off he'll be in the future with Democracy?'

Socrates pondered the idea then said,

'Naah, he wouldn't understand. The working class is always at the bottom of any system you invent.'

'Can he play football or sing and play an instrument in a boy band?', Soc asked.

Plato shook his head.

'That knocks out a career with Manchester United or Louis

---

[33] https://www.youtube.com/watch?v=4a5valsaxB8 Ken Dodd 'Happiness'

Walsh then, as well,' shrugged Soc.

'Bottom of the pile then for Xen, that's life,' he said.

Fred necked the last few drops in his glass.

'Sometimes,' he announced to the group, 'sometimes I feel like Educating Rita.'[34]

'Who's Rita?," asked Wily Sid, who'd been very interested in Fred's phone idea, looking around the pub at all the bleached blonde, spray tanned, short skirted talent on display. There was always a lot more on display on a Friday night.

Personally he had educated many of the group of females himself but scanning the group closely he couldn't place a Rita amongst them.

'She's a hairdresser from Liverpool,' said Fred by way of explanation.

'A hairdresser from Liverpool?' repeated Sid, 'You're thinking about educating a hairdresser from Liverpool?'

'Sounds like a total waste of time, if you ask me!'

Chapter 18

Wily Sid Gets Worried

Maslow's Hammer? The Conscious Incompetence Ladder? What's that all about? Pondering whether the ancient Greeks got pissed? Well, the modern ones certainly do, don't know about the oldies. Educating a hairdresser in Liverpool?

---

[34] https://www.youtube.com/watch?v=udI91Um_Z-8 Educating Rita

Whatever for?

All of these apparently disparate things were running through Sid's head and troubled him.

The new Fred who sat beside him in the lounge bar of The Edwin Waugh holding forth appeared to him to talk in riddles.

He fingered the Lower Pennines MHSU Buddies Card in his pocket, wondering if his old friend was going bonkers again, wondering whether to call Support.

Like Fred, Sid had also spent some time in the MHSU.

He was a blagger, always the can do man, getting stuff that nobody else could get, living life on the edge, ducking and diving, honing his blagging skills along the way.

It was the excitement and high from a successful blag or deal that gave him the thrill and pushed him on to the next one.

It was the shock of winning the National Lottery that sent him over the edge and into the MHSU.

It changed him from being the silver tongued skilled professional blagger persuading punters and targets to give him money.

'Always blag money off a pessimist, they don't expect it back,' he used to tell Fred or when Fred used to confide his concerns about Chardonnay to him, 'don't take life so seriously, you'll never get out of it alive, anyway.'

The Lottery Win rendered his carefully honed successful professional blagging skills wholly redundant overnight like a blacksmith without an anvil, like a Town Crier who's lost his voice.

'The worst mistake, the worst mistake I ever made,' he confided to Fred, 'was ticking the Publicity option on the Lottery Winning Claim Form.'

'It never dawned on me at the time when I was photographed taking the cheque from Bruce Forsyth that a little tick in the wrong box would totally destroy my life.'

'Everywhere I went in the town afterwards people were pointing at me as the bloke who got the big cheque from Brucie.'

'Overnight, I lost my mojo and my libido as well, thrown on the redundant skills scrapheap, a lifetime of soft skills lost to the UK Economy. All gone, the freedom of living on the edge able to move anywhere you want for new horizons, no worries about the bedroom tax, the Universal Credit or anything else.'

'Living on the streets sofa surfing and blagging is like being a developer backing their judgement. Location, location, location is the key.'

'Now I know how King Midas felt. Gold is so unsatisfying when what you really want is to bum an Americano and sticky bun bought by somebody else in Starbucks or blagged off Waitrose. Don't you agree?'

'Suddenly, I went from being a member of the undeserving poor derided by Ian Duncan Smith, to being a multi-millionaire, from having a UB40 and exchanging pleasant chats and jokes with the Jobcentre Advisor about jobs that neither she or I liked very much over a plastic cup of coffee to receiving regular threats from the Militant Tendency of the

Inland Revenue for eye watering amounts of cash, a nightmare. My life was no longer my own.'

'I've often wished that I'd simply appeared on the Lottery Publicity material as a blacked out silhouette simply holding a cheque with a strapline saying 'Lower Pennines Man scoops £5m Jackpot.'

'Overnight I changed from being an undeserving poor man to the richest man in the town, from being a hunter to the hunted.'

'You simply wouldn't believe how stressful it is to have people blagging money off you and that's not all. It's the begging letters that came in by the sack load and the Taxman.'

'Every time I answered the door bell there was a grinning Postman there with another load of mail bags.'

'Keep it going, pal!,' he would say, ' keep it going, we're all on double overtime at the Sorting Office and it's all down to you. We're all going to vote for you as Heywood Man of the Year in the Advertiser[35].'

'The missus has cancelled the coach trip and caravan at Llandudno this Summer for us and the nippers. We're all off to the Canaries this year!'

Dazed, I asked him, 'Fuerteventura? Gran Canaria? Lanzarote? Or is it Tenerife?'

'Nah, nah, nah! None of the above,' he said,' better than Tenerife.'

---

[35] Heywood Advertiser is the local paper.

Puzzled, since I'd run out of Canary Islands I waited for the Postman's reply.

'Elevenerife!,' he laughed, 'the missus has booked a big suite in a Castilla Paradore just down from the volcano with its own big pool and electric roof thing that you can move to shade if it gets too hot. You can have about 20 people on loungers under it.'

'I'm just on my way down to Thomas Cook[36] to see the video of it and put down the deposit.'

'I've told the lads on the bags and push trollies who aren't on overtime, they're welcome to come and stay. Just watch Ryanair prices for the dates, I said to them, but don't all book at once, otherwise they'll suss out that there's a big party going and put the prices up, just book in twos and threes.'

'All they'll need to bring is a sleeping bag for the loungers and a big bag of sausages and burgers from ALDI.'

'We'll have barbies, beers and singsongs every night around the pool!'

Starting up the engine, he leaned out of the window, gave Sid the thumbs' up and laughed, exclaiming,

'Isn't it great to have a few more bob around in your pocket? Isn't it great to be rich? Tirra,pal!!!'

Stunned at what I had created, I staggered back into the living room for the sanctuary and peace of the laptop, muttering to myself,

'Oh my God, oh my God, what's going on, where will it all

---

[36] https://www.thomascook.com/ Major UK Travel Agent

end?'

'No respite there though on my emails.'

'Every time I looked at my Inbox there was another load of mercenary woman chasing after my money, not my libido, on Tinder. Not wanting my libido was the real game changer for me.'

'It was that and the stress that finally triggered the breakdown with me banging on the doors of the LPMHSU and shouting to be let in,'

'No need to Section 23 me on the NHS!! I'm FREE!!! I'll go private!! I've got the loot!!!'

'Finally, peace or the beginnings of it anyway, here was a place where I could finally relax and block out the mad world which had suddenly engulfed me and taken over my entire life.'

Chapter 19

KETCHOUPP!! Street Crowdfunding

For Wily Sid, it was strolling around the LPMHSU grounds and sitting in the shade of the Lower Pennine Sculpture Park that started to get his head back into shape.

'The Who, What, Where and Whys that I exchanged with the psychologist in our regular formal and informal sessions was the beginning of a voyage of discovery about myself, who I was, what I wanted to do, where did I want to go why I wanted to change my life and restore stability in a mad world.'

'That was the real lightbulb moment.'

'Suddenly, I realised that I had the cash which I didn't want to answer all the who, what, where and why questions I was asking myself and make a permanent contribution to English society. One that would outlive me, a permanent memorial.'

'KETCHOUPP!!!'

'Keep England The Charity Home Of Undeserving Poor People!!!'

'Together, myself and the psychologist, we talked about needs, positions and personal goals. We charted out a plan of action to achieve my goals.'

'Firstly, identifying the problem. Not only had the United Kingdom lost its hard skills in fishing, mining, shipbuilding, manufacturing, steel industry and construction through the European Union, chronic Government under-investment over the years and laissez faire economics.'

'It had also lost its soft skills in the begging and blagging industries as well to foreigners with me and several others being forced off the streets by the Roma touting for cash and flogging The Big Issue.'

'There was a real problem that native soft skills honed over centuries could be lost to the United Kingdom forever with a consequential adverse knock-on effect on the economy and the GDP.'

'Then analysing the problem and sorting out a solution. Not a lot of people realise how beneficial undeserving poor people are to the UK economy and the contribution that they make to growth.'

'It's all down to middle class morality because most economists that you see on Newsnight are middle or upper class who have never begged and blagged on the street. They simply don't understand it and can't take it into account that undeserving poor people have far greater needs than poor people.'

'That's where Ian Duncan Smith has got it all wrong with Universal Credit. He thinks that undeserving poor people should have jobs whereas in the real world undeserving poor people simply want free Government cash which frees them up for begging and blagging.'

'You see, poor people don't make the contribution to the UK economy and the GDP that undeserving poor people make.'

'Poor people are grateful for a bag of old Primark clothes which don't fit and a box of own label tins of beans from the Trussell Trust Foodbank and have to write a grovelling thank you note to the Chair of the Middle Class Charity Committee for getting them.'

'Undeserving poor people don't need or want old clothes or cheap beans because their needs and wants are far greater than poor people and they never write letters to middle class Chairs or anyone else.'

'Why cut down forests damaging the Green Agenda creating more carbon dioxide to provide paper to write thank you letters? It's far easier, faster, more immediate and personal when you can simply text Authority with a 'Ta, mate for the dosh' message and a Selfie to identify yourself from your latest iPhone 6?'

'If you hobble undeserving poor people with jobs they don't want coupled with 19th century middle class charity, morality and letters then you flat line the economy, destroy the British begging and blagging service industries which have taken centuries to build up and fine tune to their current world class position and in the process you create a vacuum into which the Roma and others step into with a vastly inferior product and service.'

'In addition they overcrowd doctors' surgeries and schools and colleges which undeserving poor people don't bother with much pushing up NHS and public spending.'

'What undeserving poor people need and want is the latest Tommy Hilfiger, Diesel or Berghaus leisure wear, an account at the local Curry House for home delivery, a decent brand 50" Smart HDTV for *Strictly Come Dancing*, *The Great British Bake Off*, *I'm a Celebrity*.'

'They need at least a 6 month Sky Sports Subscription to watch England get beaten again on penalties by the Germans in the Euros with a £100 Boozebuster Voucher thrown in for the Stella Artois, partially paid for by Universal Credit, topped up through begging and blagging on the street.'

'That's the way to keep ahead of the curve and maintain England's world class reputation and position right at the cutting edge of being the No.1 destination of choice for undeserving poor people.'

'A great boost to the retail sector of the economy and that's where KETCHOUPP!!! comes in.'

'Our market research carried out at big sportswear SuperStores and social housing schemes established that a Gift Voucher for about £250 of Tommy Hilfiger stuff shoved in the pocket of a set of joggers or through selected letterboxes, the ones with a Sky dish and a nearly new SUV 4 x 4 on the front drive or on the pavement worked best.'

'That was about the median rate that an undeserving poor person would need to get them started.'

'That satisfied the needs bit but we had to address the aspiration, motivation and blagging side of things as well, so how to do it?'

'The best test results came from part payment vouchers and rebranding. Begging and blagging are so old and dated name labels with their 19th century charity connotations.'

'Well, a part payment voucher system showed the best results, use the £250 Tommy Hilfiger voucher against £400 worth of clothing with them having to blag the extra £150 off somebody else.'

'Putting it all in place. That's how we worked out who the best future prospects were for blagging to carry KETCHOUPP!! into the future. From the names and addresses on the vouchers as they were used and received back at HQ, we selected a group of 50 who looked the best prospects for training in the necessary soft skills and had a Dragon's Den type format to wheedle the numbers down.'

'Rebranding was the big paradigm change. Begging and blagging is so 19th century conjuring up images of stern Victorians presiding over requests from poor people for pittances to scrape by.'

'We needed a new identity to describe what it was in 21st century England, to emphasise the great contribution made by undeserving poor people to the UK economy, particularly the retail trade.'

'Street Crowdfunding captured the essential spirit of what we were trying to achieve. All of our graduates from the Dragon Den's format wore snazzy eye catching uniform leisure tops carrying the strapline 'I'm NOT what you think, I'm a Street Crowdfunder'.

'Fully equipped with logos and professional printed boards with iphone6s and PayPal Card Machine readers, our graduates were ready for the challenge of putting a fully professional front on Street Crowdfunding.'

'Able to flashmob Roma beggars with their plastic coffee cups badly written cardboard signs and Big Issues out of existence and put UK Street Crowdfunding ahead of the curve to keep England at the top of its charity game.'

'I was getting acres more newsprint than White Dee in The Sun and Daily Mail.'

'Their training with KETCHOUPP!! solved their job application requirement with the DWP Advisor.'

'Scalability of the solution. Once we'd got the regional model sorted, it was time to go national then international starting with Magaluf.'

'It was Tristram, a struck off solicitor on the KETCHOUPP!! Board who spotted the Magaluf angle, big resident British population, apartments and hotels often built illegally without planning permissions etc.

'So we bunged in a wad of readies to buy a block of apartments right on the Mediterranean, all with sea views, built without permissions with a good chance of being demolished.

'A real beauty, offering All You Can Eat buffets, with direct access on the ground floor off the beach to The Crafty Cockney 24 hour Sports Bar with wall to wall TVs and a fast access lift after you'd stuffed yourself stupid to The Lancashire Laddie Roof Top Open Bar for late night singsongs'

"Ooooh!... the memories of a football singsong."

Ooooooh, mey lads.

You should have seen their faces,

Walking down the Warwick Rooooad!!!,

To see Sir Alec's Aces!!

J.S. Park! J.S. Park!,
He'll eat anything that has a bark,

Buuuuut, it's better he's Korean and not a Scouse,
Or he'd have to eat rats in his Council House!!"

From the banks of the River Irwell
To the shores of Sicily,
We will fight, fight, fight for United,
'Til we win the Champions' League

Glory, glory, Man United,
Glory, glory, Man United,
Glory, glory, Man United,
And the reds go marching on, on, on...

They were always Manchester United chants and songs.

'You would never think that it might all come to an end, the chanting, the singing, the camaraderie, the long lazy days, and the sun slipping slowly over the horizon into the Med.'

Chapter 20

Guerilla Gardening

Standing in the undergrowth around PASTELLS, Fred addressed his new group of trainees in Guerilla Gardening, all in their second week, apart from a new starter.

'Weeds,' he said, 'are our enemies. They're far smarter than proper plants, they crawl along the ground, sneak in amongst our plants, grow on their fertiliser, and carry their seeds on the wind.'

'It's eternal vigilance, checking, looking for them, it's like illegal immigrants. So how do we stop them from getting into our beds?', looking at the group.

'Vote UKIP,' said the new starter.

Fred glared, and mentally marked him down for an Equality & Diversity training session.

'Pull, throw and dig! Pull, throw and dig!' shouted Fred, showing the technique.

Soon the line of trainees was moving backwards in unison, the area of brown rich soil started to expand and a sizeable heap of weeds was starting to rise behind the potting shed for compost next year.

At home, Fred had started on his Recycling for Alternative Technology project. He had linked up his stock of redundant Tyrolean Projectors with a PIR as an alternative Burglar Deterrent Alarm. From his Army days, he'd rigged them up in a diamond formation. When the 1000 watt PIR was activated, they fired non-stop into the killing theatre.

The blinding light would dazzle any one, who would then be bombarded by stones being fired from all directions.

Fred was pleased with his handiwork. It had taken about half a day to set up and fine tune.

Satisfied that everything worked, Fred now believed he had the best protected, burglar proof house in the neighbourhood and put a Post It on his Smartphone to send to the local Neighbourhood Police Officer later, before heading off to the Edwin Waugh.

Mrs. Lloyd George-Varley had been Chair of the Lower Pennines Conservative Group for ten years and had honed it into a modern lean political force gaining seats and cutting Council Tax every year.

Her name had obviously helped.

'Yes,' she said, anticipating the frequent question, 'He was my great, great, grand uncle, twice removed. Just call me LGV.'

Actually the Labour opposition called her Transit[37] because of her generously proportioned backside.

Her success in such a Tory wilderness had caught the eye of Central Office who had marked her in as a future Parliamentary candidate.

Flushed with her success at pushing through local fracking and giving free phone calls through the DTPECO initiative, the Pennine Foundry had started to increase its workforce and introduced overtime for the first time in years.

---

[37] Transit is a Ford van. LGV is short for Light Goods Vehicle.

The call from the Downing Street Policy Officer that Grant the Chairman was coming for photo ops with her at PASTELLS sent her walking in the clouds with pride.

'How ironic,' she laughed to herself. Downing Street had spotted a Green newspaper piece in the Guardian about PASTELLS excellent multiskilling and recycling.

The bloody Guardian of all papers praising a Conservative Council she thought.

- A model to be followed on community development with low unemployment, no foodbanks needed here and food miles decimated, with the excellent fresh produce available from Fred's Guerrilla Gardening spots all over the town and a 75% decrease in the carbon footprint and food miles .....

Fred and Daphne had become even closer with preparations for the visit.

The Guerilla Gardening area was heaving with luscious produce which was now partly being harvested for the buffet dinner.

Fred had started to experiment with cooking and had used Daphne's Cooking for One recipes to work out quantities of produce required.

It took the guesswork out. You simply multiplied it by the expected numbers for the buffet, so easy.

Sid had roped in Nick and Besharat as well with a pop up bar and Afghan tasting restaurant. It was part of his Discover Afghanistan initiative.

He reckoned that before the present conflict and television

reports from Helmand Province all that most people knew about this distant faraway remote country was that it was the origin of Afghan coats popular with hippies and flower power people in the 1960s and Afghan Hounds.

About its food and culture people knew nothing.

This was an opportunity for Sid to get in first ahead of the herd for the expected flood of interest in Afghanistan that occasions such as this would generate.

Together with BertMI6 with his IT and electronics experience, he had designed a digital collar for Afghan Hounds which could be set to beep 5 times a night to wake them up for walks and prayers.

There were testing trays of Besharat's Abghoost all around with a generous supply of their established Monkeytown and Moonraker brews to wash it down.

For the special occasion Nick had also produced a Limited Edition new brew.

Pen9 dark beer, at 9% alcohol by volume, was the strongest beer on the market.

Chapter 21

The Great Day

The great day arrived and PASTELLS was a hub of activity.

Fred was so busy at setting things up with trainees fitted out with new clean overalls, catering staff in whites and food being cooked and displayed, checking for stray weeds with visitors milling around that he'd no time to help Daphne who he reckoned was probably out of sight somewhere, busy with her Art and Sculpture with the two Italians who were at the Centre on the ERASMUS programme to work in and experience the British way of working and culture.

It was Darren who told him that Daphne was in the local A & E with concussion.

Apparently, she'd called round to Fred's house for last minute thoughts and ideas, found Fred was out and had been attacked by yobs who'd blinded her with a bright light then pelted her with stones when she'd taken a short cut through his back garden to her car.

Oh, Christ!- thought Fred, he'd forgotten to tell her about his Alternative Burglar Alarm system using the Tyrolean Projectors.

It was time for the photo shots with Conservative Central Office.

There was the Chair on the left, LGV in the middle and Fred on the right, all beaming with a glass of champagne in hand on the raised dais.

'Britain is back in the game with a Conservative government,' announced the Chair to the assembled TV, press and photographers, ' PASTELLS has shown what a forward looking Conservative local administration can achieve in the Labour wastelands of the Lower Pennines....reskilling with new skills and training...with almost full employment locally, producing local food for local people eliminating food miles and slashing energy costs with fracking.'

He flourished a sheet of paper in the air that he had been given by the Policy Officer.

'..and it's not just reskilling, new jobs and local food production. It's day tripper tourists as well coming to PASTELLS Guerilla Gardens. I have here the latest day tripper hotspots from the United Kingdom Alternative Tourism Guide.'

'In number three position we have Hog's Back Puttenham in Surrey, in number two position we have Mole Valley in Reigate and in number one position is PASTELLS Guerilla Gardens in the Lower Pennines."

'That's proof positive that a local Conservative administration has closed the North-South gap.'

LGV beamed at this news about which she had not been previously aware.

'It only came into the Policy Office this morning before I left London,' said the Chair to her.

All three raised their glasses to their lips for the photo shoot.

LGV had indulged very freely on Besharat's Abghoost tasters washed down with Nick's Limited Edition Pen9 craft beer as well as Fred's traditional buffet offerings.

She turned to Fred and said,

'That was an excellent buffet (*hic!*), Fred, the various cold meats, (*hic!*) which ones did you use?'

'Mainly Roadkill,' said Fred, 'Foxes, hedgehogs, rabbits, badgers and so on.'

LGV's face suddenly froze, went white, turned green, then with glass to lips, she suddenly felt very sick with dark brown vomit spattering over the Press.

The photographer from Socialist Worker caught her in full flight. It was on next week's front page. A large picture of LGV, glass to lips, projectiley vomiting with the strapline below the photograph saying LOCAL TORY SAYS FRACKING NOT DANGEROUS TO DRINKING WATER.

Its' other main story was about the United Kingdom Alternative Tourism Guide where PASTELLS Guerilla Gardens had taken the top spot. Apparently it was a list of the most popular dogging spots in the UK.

After the chaos of the reception, Fred finally managed to clean and lock up and headed off to the A&E to see Daphne to update her on the disaster that had befallen him.

Daphne was sat up in bed in the cubicle with a red bandage around her head looking slightly like Che Guevara.

'Tell me more about the United Kingdom Alternative Tourism Guide and PASTELLS Guerilla Gardens being the number one dogging spot in the UK,' she said, grasping Fred's arm and pulling him closer.

She was working on a new free course for the Open University Future Learning programme on sexual practices.

This would make a fascinating local input into it.

She saw it all in her head as Fred expounded on the day's events.

'Yes, yes, yes!!' she shouted excitedly, 'I've just thought of the course title that I want,' she declared, pulling Fred down on to the hospital bed.

'I'm going to call it Sexual Practices Down the Centuries – The road from Athens to Magaluf via the Lower Pennines..'

Chapter 22

The Aftermath

The disasters of the Great Day had taken their toll and had deeply depressed Fred.

Mrs. Lloyd George Varley appearing in full colour throwing up on the front page of the Socialist Worker coupled with the duplicitous use of the photograph linking it with the dangers of fracking to the water supply and the sheer embarrassment, unknown to him, of having created the United Kingdom's No. 1 dogging spot were all hammer blows which wounded him deeply.

There was a big enquiry by the Management Committee into all of the planning and events which had been put in place for The Great Day, how the various disasters had come about with the aim of putting together recommendations for the future.

The first rule in any public enquiry and the PASTELLS Management Committee investigation was no different, is to find someone to blame for the disaster.

Fred, because he had been so prominent in getting things together, started to get the distinct feeling that he was being scapegoated by the Management Committee for everything which had happened and gone wrong and went on an extended sick leave from PASTELLS.

The final nail in his depressed state was his lead handsets.

His other great idea of Free Phone Calls for the Elderly had also come to a shuddering halt. All the handsets had been nicked in one fell swoop, it was on Crimewatch.

The Local Authority CCTV system had managed to catch a few poor images of someone cutting off all the lead handsets across the Town Centre. When he saw the video shots on the TV with a Police Contact telephone number running across the bottom of the picture he thought that the shadowy figure seen running away looked slightly like Wily Sid, but immediately cast the thought out of his mind.

But set against all these knocks to his ego, there was Daphne. In a life suddenly full of negatives she was a distinct positive.

Daphne was the only bright spot in his life.

After she'd been released from the hospital following her recovery from concussion and a full head examination, she had decided to come to Fred's house, at his insistence, for a few days rest and recuperation.

The few days stretched into a few weeks.

They were lying together upstairs in each other's arms when it happened.

There was a loud knocking on the front door.

Hurriedly, Fred rose out bed, couldn't see what was happening through the window, so he donned his dressing gown and went downstairs to see who it was.

He pulled the front door open.

A slim, tanned blonde woman with her back to him was standing on the doorstep, hand in hand with a small boy dressed in a Superman uniform. She was giving instructions on where to stack all the stuff to the driver unloading luggage and boxes from the van on the road.

She turned around.

 It was Chardonnay.

The shock of seeing his wife standing there on the front door step was simply too much for Fred to take in all at once.

She looked calmly at him staggering back into the hall, knocking over one of Daphne's Greek urns which stood there, scattering the Pampas grasses onto the wooden floor.

She nodded down at the small boy, holding her hand, looked back at Fred and then exclaimed,

'E's yours, your nipper, we're back from Spain. Wayne, say hello to your Dad.'

Daphne heard the voices, the crash of the urn and jumped out of the bed.

She grabbed the first thing at hand, a colourful touristy bath towel, pulled it around her and started down the stairs to see what was going on below.

The two women's eyes met in mutual recognition

'Daph Crabtree!' yelled Chardonnay, 'Ye bleeding slapper!! And you're wearing my Benidorm towel as well!!. Give it back here!!'

The two women struggled in the hall as a dazed Fred staggered into the front room and went to sit on one of the boxes unloaded by the driver.

'Gerroff!' the small boy called out to Fred, 'That's mey mam's

LLadro stuff in there.' and pushed Fred off the box towards the open door.

The small boy studied his mother and Daphne pushing and grabbing each other and made an instant decision on what to do.

Hurling himself forward he suddenly shouted,

'Superman to the rescue!' and grabbed Daphne's leg sinking his teeth into it.

All three, Chardonnay, Daphne and Superman ended up in the front garden followed by Fred.

Just then the two Italians, Berlo and Nero, arrived on the scene. They had come to the end of their ERASMUS placement and popped around to say their final farewells to Fred and Daphne.

'Aaah Vred, Defne,' said Berlo, with a wide grin on his face watching the two women fighting over Chardonnay's Benidorm beach towel and what remained of Daphne's underwear, 'I have 'eard of zee English street partees, but I nevair knew zee were bunga bunga partees !!'

Berlo removed his shirt slowly, exposing his oiled clean shaven chest and passed it to Daphne to cover up her embarrassment.

Together, arm in arm, all three of them, Berlo, a tearful Daphne and Nero retreated back up the street.

'That'll be £5.60 for the week,' said the milkman on his evening collection round to Fred, looking at Daphne's pale blue Ann Summer's bra hanging from the tree, floating in the breeze.

'Pheeeew!! Just like a Manchester City banner in the good old days when they played at Maine Road with no Arab money behind them,' he thought, 'no cups and no support.'

Chapter 23

Diamond is a Girl's Best Friend

After a tumultuous start which even involved an application to appear on the Jeremy Kyle Show, things settled down into a routine between Fred and Chardonnay.

After the rows, threats and accusations both ways they recognised that there was fault on both sides, Fred with Daphne, Chardonnay with the Bingo Bingo Manager.

Both had departed the scene, Daphne to Tuscany with Nero, the Bingo Bingo Manager shortly after discovering Chardonnay was pregnant. Luckily, the apartment that they'd got in Magaluf had a largely British presence in the blocks with two bars. The Crafty Cockney on the ground floor and The Lancashire Laddie on the rooftop.

Fending for herself, the mainly British blocks gave her a regular clientele to revive her Avon Calling! Party Plan business which had come to an abrupt halt in rural under populated North Yorkshire at Catterick and she had also started to sell on eBay.

The Party Plan business brought back her confidence in her selling and presentational skills and soon she'd added the package tour welcome meetings in The Crafty Cockney to her regular venues.

Business thrived over the high season and ticked over nicely in the winter months. The eBay online business grew steadily and confirmed her ability to spot emerging trends and get in there first for super profits before the herd noticed what was trending. By then she had already moved on to the next big seller.

Everything on the eBay online business was on the up with a steadily rising sales and profit line on the graph, pushed onwards and upwards by great Feedback from buyers… Yellow, Blue, Turquoise and Purple ratings were easily achieved within the first year from the resident Brits in the blocks, a lull then the High Season visitors next year pushed her past the 1,000 Good Feedback mark into the Red Star zone.

With positive Feedback ratings never slipping below the high 90% ages she was heading for UK Powerseller status to join the aristocracy of eBay.

This was only if she returned and based her business in the United Kingdom. It was something she was actively considering.

Business was taking off again this year. The next Alpine peak of 4,999 was becoming visible and she was already well up into its' foothills.

Then it all came shuddering to a halt.

As she was setting up her presentation in the Crafty Cockney she looked at the three letters she'd picked up from her Inbox.

The first was a leaflet from Conservatives Abroad.

'High taxes in the UK!! NO, NO, NO. The British people live under a tax cutting Conservative Government. Revving up in the fast lane of the World Economy, the UK had the fastest growth rate of large industrial countries, neck and neck with the US shouting 'Out of my way! out of my way!'

'We're leaving the Germans panting in our wake, struggling to read our rear screen sticker - Go and rebuild your bloody wall again'.

'The French, Italians etc. are so far behind, you can scarcely see them in the rear mirror.'

'Britain is very much back in the game!! So why not join us if you're thinking of returning to the UK? or back us with a Donation to carry on the good work of making Britain Great again?"

The other two were from the Municipalatie and the local Ayuntamiento, they were both in red and in Spanish, not just ordinary Spanish but official Spanish which she struggled to understand.

There had been a meeting with all the residents about 4 weeks previously which had been addressed by a representative of the owners, a bloke called Tristram.

Apparently, the blocks had all been built without full planning permission. But as he pointed out, so had most of the resort.

There was no reason why the Municipalitie or Ayuntamieno should choose their blocks to demolish, if indeed they intended to demolish illegal buildings over other illegal blocks and hotels.

Others were not so sure.....their blocks were the only British owned blocks ..the others were all Spanish owned. Their blocks also had a top class prime location right on the beach.

They were right.

While trying to decipher what the Spanish letters said … Chardonnay was disturbed by one of the other residents.

The British blocks were scheduled for demolition today.

The Spanish workmen for the Municipalatie and Ayuntamiento had already entered the blocks and had started to put up shuttering over the windows of The Crafty Cockney to prevent re-occupation …once the block had been cleared.

She was luckier than most. The bulk of her eBay local stock was in a small warehouse complex which was not affected by the demolition order at the rear of the blocks…. most of her international eBay sales were dropshipped from the United Kingdom.

The shuttering and the letter from Conservatives Abroad made her mind up, it was back to the United Kingdom.

With her neighbour from Leeds, they both packed up their belongings from their apartments and warehouse complex and filled the Mercedes HiTop Van which Chardonnay had used for local deliveries.

She picked up Wayne from the English International School and started on the long journey by ferry from Alcudia to Barcelona, then driving through Northern Spain and France to Calais then Dover.

She wondered what she was moving back to as the distance for The North and the Lower Pennines decreased along the M1.

With the departure of the Bingo Bingo Manager and Daphne

out of both Chardonnay and Fred's lives, after the initial traumatic days when Jeremy Kyle had been contacted, things started to settle down.

Together, they decided to put it all in the past, close the folder on the past and make a fresh start.

They basically discovered each other once again.

With being off on the sick, Fred started to become more involved in Chardonnay's online business, packaging up goods, putting up racking for storage and streamlining the IT side of things to make the business a sleek 24hour operation.

Selling goods, with the printer springing into life regularly throughout the night producing address labels and despatch notes, as they slept, ready for order picking the following day achieved the 'always open for business aims.'

That was when Fred had his lightbulb moment.

He had long felt that Chardonnay's website of simple listings was old fashioned.

What it lacked, he felt, was a focal point, a unique selling point to draw in the punters who were scrolling through the listings of beauty products.

He had discussed his thoughts with BertMI6, drawing on his extensive IT experience, which had been so useful in the SuperStore token Special Ops targeting web shoppers.

BertMI6 was pleased to help and sent him some coding patches[38] to put his plans into operation.

---

[38] http://oss-watch.ac.uk/resources/softwarepatch Code Patching

With his experience in Strategy, Tactics and Operations …
Fred felt it needed the Diamond formation, to channel buyers
into the killing zone, the focal point and make a financial
bonanza.

With Chardonnay asleep he started on the task of
remodelling the website to what he knew would work, as it
had done during his military and shop security careers.

With the job done applying BertMI6's patches he moved the
site from offline to live. He didn't have time for a full test run
through to check that everything ran as normal.[39]

He fingered the Jeremy Kyle contact card and put a Post It
note on his Smartphone to remind him to ring his studio PA
tomorrow and cancel their scheduled appearance on the
show.

The job completed, he turned the lights off and slipped into
bed beside Chardonnay.He was rudely awoken by
Chardonnay screaming at about 7.00am.

She was always up early to check on the overnight sales.

'Oh my God, OH MY GOD .. OH MY GAWD!!!!! What the
bleeding hell have you done with my website???,' she
screamed at him, whacking him around the head.

The Jeremy Kyle Show was back top of the agenda.

Chapter 24

Sid Gets Job Satisfaction

---

[39] https://en.wikipedia.org/wiki/Regression_testing Regression Testing

Wily Sid lay back on Nick's settee and lit a cigarette.

He was satisfied.

He had achieved his purpose.

His libido was back fully functioning, fully proven by his earlier one to one that he had with an attractive blonde from the Edwin Waugh.

All that National Lottery cash and subsequent publicity that had blighted his life, his libido and caused his mental breakdown through the stress of suddenly becoming the richest man in the Lower Pennines and being pursued for money, money, money all the time had thankfully disappeared in the dust and rubble of Magaluf.

He was like Brewster, in Brewster's Millions, trying to lose every single cent of his cash challenge in order to meet his goal and inherit his millions.

Sid had achieved his goal as well, by losing all of his as he had planned.

The goal of liberty as a free Englishman, free of cash that he hadn't wanted, free from being stalked for money, free from avaricious women on Tinder pursuing him for it, was now his.

He was his own man once more, free once more to pursue what was in his genes, what he was brought up to do, free to blag.

His new job as Merchandising Manager at SuperStore had gone mental because of the constant swarming of crowds of mercenary women chasing him and crowds pointing at him through the shop windows.

He thought to himself that there is really nothing more innately satisfying to do than something which you are born into and which you are very good at.

He had recaptured England's pole position for the undeserving poor with KETCHOUPP!!

KETCHOUPP!! Keep England The Charity Home Of Undeserving Poor People was now firmly embedded in the British consciousness and also in the Big Society.

KETCHOUPP!! was his finest achievement, he felt.

It was his Richard the Lionheart moment.

There was no need nowadays to pursue England's enemies all the way down through France, pausing to burn Joan of Arc at the stake on the way, then to Spain and back over the Mediterranean to Arabia.

In the 21st century dealing with different hostiles in the form of Eastern European beggars you outblagged them with KETCHOUPP!! Street Crowdfunding and flash mobs.

You simply chased them on to budget airline flights to Bucharest, Bratislava etc., heading back in the general direction of where they had originally come from.

With a free Terranova Bus Ticket to somewhere pretty dreadful and a charity Scratchcard, these would serve to remind them of the essential basic humanity of the United Kingdom.

He reflected that if budget airlines had been around in the time of Richard the Lionheart, life for the King would have been so much simpler and easier in chasing hostiles.

He was not directly involved in the day to day activities of KETCHOUPP!! Street Crowdfunding any more as unpaid non-Executive Chairman.

It was Tristram and BertMI6 who now had executive control of the organisation.

He blew another very satisfying smoke ring into the air and reflected that not many people have an idea which morphs into a movement which achieved both national and international importance of spreading English soft skills in blagging far and wide.

It was now also being backed and promoted by the British Council and the Department for International Development as part of their joint Understanding Britain programme for overseas aid and development.

He dwelled on how his early life prior to joining the regular Army had helped.

He smiled to himself at the memory and where it had led him.

After detaching himself from day to day management of KETCHOUPP!! he was able to revive his career as a blagger, always one to spot an opportunity.

He was in the early, very successful stages of forging a night career as well to supplement his SuperStore daytime job and Street Crowdfunding.

It was a training course with NECAARSE (Next Careers After Army Service) funded by non-other than HRH (Help for Returning Heroes) which had set him on his new night time career as a New Age comedian successfully finding himself a niche in the comedy market in Greater Manchester.

Life was looking up again.

Chapter 25

Life's not always a Drag

A void existed between the new alternative comedy spots in Central Manchester at Deansgate Locks where numerous very forgettable wannabee performers told their unfunny tales and jokes (?) and the traditional politically incorrect, but laugh out loud, suburban and very funny venues like Bernard Manning's Embassy Club[40] or Frankie Lamar's Foo Foo's Palace,[41] in the City Centre, specialising in drag.

Both venues were now left bereft because of the deaths of their mainstays.

Sid's old Army colleague Nick had restarted drag

Sid and Nick had tried to bridge the gap in their act which was being increasingly well-received.

In his Army fatigues, Sid could take the stage in either market and get a good reception.

'I met a transvestite in Manchester City Centre today, he had a Wigan address.'

'War heroes! War heroes!' he could shout, to the dimly lit audience,

'Tonight we have real war heroes in the audience,' waving towards the rear where Nick and Besharat were sitting.

---

[40] https://www.youtube.com/watch?v=JIHN1UkcSGo Bernard Manning
[41] https://www.youtube.com/watch?v=npQjaXG1HWs Foo Foo Lamar

When the crowd applauded and looked, both Nick and Besharat would stand up in their Afghan dress and he would then add,

'They're both Taliban, so if you wanna' clap for them like that!!!, ….then I don't know!...where have we gone wrong.'

There was an Englishman, an Irishman and an Afghan, all standing at the bar drinking, and the barman says,

'Is this a joke?' or the alternative

There was an Englishman, an Irishman and an Afghan, all standing at the bar drinking,

'What a wonderful example of UK multi-cultural society!'

There was a group of English, Irish, French, German, Japanese, American, Moroccan, Jamaican, Mongolian, Russian, Ukrainian men all standing outside a Night Club in the City Centre and the Doorman said, 'You can't come in here!!! You need a Thai!'

'Geordies must be totally confused that Allday (Geordie pronunciation of Aldi) isn't open 24 hours a day.'

My driving test examiner said to me on the test,

'Can you pull over somewhere when it's safe and we'll do the Highway Code symbols test?'

Ten minutes later, I was still driving along the road and he frowned over his clipboard with the signs on it and said, 'Why haven't you pulled over yet?'

I said, "We're still in Liverpool!"

'The national anthem of Libyan asylum seekers?'

'Row, row, row your boat.'

It was wrongfooting the audience with stereotypes and they loved it.

.

As he lay on the settee, he glanced across at the selection of glamour dresses and wigs that Nick, whose house he was in, had acquired over time for his drag act, and smiled at the memory of Nick's drag jokes.

'You've got a gorgeous head on your shoulders, Luv, but it would be better on a neck.'

'Your friend's so ugly she hands out whistles to builders.'

Chapter 26

Nick's Tribunal Hearing

Gunner Nick Smith had started in drag by chance when he had decided that a shortened Army Career by way of a Medical Discharge would suit him better than seeing out the full 10 years that he had signed up for.

Inspired by Corporal Klinger in the US Television Series M*A*S*H[42] who took to wearing female clothing in order to try and get a Section 8 discharge from the United States military, that of a member judged mentally unfit for service, Nick had started to do exactly the same.

Whereas the fictional series M*A*SH was set in the mid-20th Century 1950s Korean War, Nick's war was firmly in the early 21st Century with a huge attitude change having taken place in the preceding 60 years.

---

[42] https://en.wikipedia.org/wiki/M*A*S*H_(TV_series) M*A*S*H

Nick's behaviour in insisting on wearing female clothing at all times soon brought him up on a charge. For his appearance before the Military Disciplinary Tribunal, he had chosen a fetching red dress with a plunging neckline which he'd got from ASOS.[43]

The Hearing was in the traditional format with three officers sitting behind a table.

Nick was represented by another officer.

The Sergeant Major hovered around in the background, not taking part in proceedings, but available to answer any questions on Nick, his attitudes and how he fitted in with colleagues which might arise from the Tribunal.

The Sergeant Major had a traditional view of Army life and discipline but wearily accepted the new views on sexuality and human rights seeping in from civilian life.

He looked at the three officers sitting on judgement on Nick and reflected on the old British Army dictum and how true it was,

' All officers are like babies, they all look the bloody same!'.

The Disciplinary Hearing was now in Session.

It was chaired by Major 'Pongo' de Gascoigne-Wetherley. Pongo came from a long family line of military service. He could draw on his long family experience of military service stretching back numerous generations.

Before the Disciplinary Hearing he reflected on this and jokingly said to the other two Tribunal members 'that my great, great grandfather had probably presided over similar

---

[43] www.**asos**.com High fashion online retailer.

miscreants in the original Anglo Afghan wars of the 19th century.'

'Quite,' said Captain 1.
'Indeed,' said Captain 2, 'but military life has changed somewhat in the interim.'

'Indeed, it has,' agreed 'Pongo', in my great, great grandfather's day, he'd simply have been cashiered out of the regiment and that would have been that.'

'But, we live and soldier in different times now with civilian human rights legislation having pushed its way into military life and we have to take that into account in our decision.'

The Tribunal heard both the supporting and opposing arguments put forward on Nick's behaviour.

'Pongo' asked for any views that the Sergeant Major might have on Nick before the Tribunal retired to consider their decision.

The Sergeant Major looked at Nick in his high fashion red dress with a look of disgust and said,

'Well, Pon.. sorry, Sah!!, he's no Joanna Lumley, that's for sure, sah!!'

The Tribunal retired.

It wasn't long before they returned to announce their decision.

The Major laid out the reasons for their decision and how they had arrived at it.

'Firstly,' the Major said,' we are a fighting force, clothed and armed as such, in a uniformed military style, recognisable as such by those who oppose us and those we seek to protect. That is our prime role.'

'Secondly, we do not exist in a vacuum. We must perform our prime role against a background of duties and responsibilities laid upon us by a civilian government which reflects the culture of the society from which we all come which is dynamic in constant change.'

'Our decision therefore reflects both these two functions.'

'We therefore find that Gunner Smith does have the right to wear female clothing as is his personal choice but it must be of a type which is culturally appropriate to the environment in which we are operating.'

'Gunner Smith must therefore wear either a Pashtun dress or light thin cotton trousers with a belted kamis shirt. Outside of base he must wear a burqa or a niqab.'

'That is the decision of this Tribunal.'

'All rise,' shouted the Sergeant Major.

With his can do attitude and ability to source difficult to find items, Sid was despatched to the local market to purchase suitable clothing for Nick.

Triumphantly, he returned to base with an armful of gaudy embroidered female clothing and niqabs with a gauze panel completely covering the eye slit.

Nick lasted in his outfits for less than three weeks before giving up on his quest for discharge. He couldn't stand the banging headaches he was getting from attempting to look through the gauze material of the niqab sight panel.

Everywhere he looked after taking it off he was seeing squares.

He packed up all his dresses and accessories in a trunk in his quarters and settled down to see out the 10 years he had signed up for.

The Defence Review making him redundant was his saviour.

Chapter 27

Bert's Grand Strategy

BertMI6 smiled to himself at how his plans had worked out since he had left the Regular Army.

He had always prided himself on his ability to spot and develop talent in the operatives who worked under him in the murky world of Special Ops.

Sometimes you needed someone who was rigid and inflexible and never deviated from the plan, at other times you needed someone with the ability to improvise on the spot and flex the plan to changing circumstances.

Fred and Sid were two totally different characters.

Fred needed certainty and fixed points. He could only work to the plan.

Sid could think on his feet and adapt the Strategy, Tactics and Operations in the plan to meet a new development. His acting background helped as did his ability to read a situation and nuance the plan to fit. He was an improviser.

His background in Special Ops with emphasis on Strategy, Tactics and Operations had transferred so easily to the private sector.

Both types of personalities were needed to make Special Ops work.

The success of the Special Ops concepts in transferring so well to the private sector was largely down to Fred still working to plan with a military mindset in the civilian world.

Special Ops was split between Black Ops, Grey Ops and White Ops, often overlapping each other.

Black Ops were overt operations with the key features of being secret and not attributable to the organization carrying it out with a significant degree of deception, to conceal who is behind it or to make it appear that some other entity is responsible e.g. false flag.

Fred's identification of web shopping as a major threat to BASSTARDS and BertMI6's response with vouchers which wouldn't print together with time dated tokens with were almost impossible to use because of their short usable lifespan were classic Black Ops scenarios. Blame was directed towards the voucher and token providers not SuperStore when they couldn't be used.

It was a similar success story on kettling, putting all paying customers in one queue for the tills developed from the British Army 'protected villages' experience in Malaya, thus clearing the floor for Security surveillance and Profiling.

The Malayan 'protected village' in military terms simply meant rounding up all the locals not involved in terrorism within a guarded encampment where they were well looked after.

Anyone found outside in the jungle by army patrols was

assumed to be a terrorist and simply shot.[44]

Adapting it to the retail world meant putting all shoppers in the 'protected village' of the kettling[45] single queue looked after by Sid, feeding them samples of Abghoost and small glasses of Nick's craft beers.

Anyone not in the single queue could then be closely scrutinised and screened by Fred, his choppers and Diamond in Store Security.

'Were they genuine shoppers who would subsequently take their place in the kettling queue or were they hostiles and fellow travellers out to disrupt store operations and Diamond?'

A grey op presented as helping customers to avoid slow and problem shoppers at tills but which actually weeded them out to concentrate better on the hostiles and fellow travellers.

His favourite Special Op was the white op dreamed up by Sid with his lottery win and his fake declared intention of giving it all away. Placing Sid in SuperStore as Merchandising Manager was a magnet for customers hoping to get a share of the dosh that Sid was pretending to get rid of as fast as possible.

The constant heaving crowds outside the store meant more footfall, more shoppers, more sales, more profit, more security staff and more members for BASSTARDS.

He had moved aside from the day to day operations of BASSTARDS and spun off a subsidiary wholly owned by himself to commercially exploit new retail security ideas

---

[44] https://en.wikipedia.org/wiki/Briggs%27_Plan The Briggs Plan
[45] https://en.wikipedia.org/wiki/Kettling What is kettling ?

which had come up on the BASSTARDS Facebook page and been shown to work.

His subsidiary was PBP PTIPTO Plc. (Profit Before People Pull Them In Push Them Out).

What PBP offered was a retail security and promotional service based on proven strategies backed up by military precision targeted Special Ops which worked.

Aside from PBP, he had joined the Executive Board of KETCHOUPP!! at Sid's invitation.

He smiled to himself again as he surveyed his business interests thinking,

'It was all initially down to Fred's chopper and Diamond formation.'

When a feature about PBP PTIPTO and its services appeared in The Grocer, it elicited a wide response from the retail trade.

He even got a call from two of the Dragons from Dragons' Den[46] who had seen the article and were intrigued by the huge profit increase that his methods had helped to create.

They wanted to buy 40% for £500,000 without even seeing the books or carrying out due diligence.

He later discovered from his phone records that it was Sid with his gift for mimicry and acting background who had made the calls and smiled to himself…he would have done exactly the same if he had Sid's skills.

Testing each other and testing each other's strategies was

---

[46] http://www.bbc.co.uk/programmes/b006vq92 Popular BBC TV Show

part and parcel of Special Ops.

If your colleague could fool you into disclosure, your enemy could do exactly the same. It was a proven method of testing new strategies to ensure they were watertight.

BertMI6 always monitored his own calls and those of his colleagues as well. You never took anything for granted in Ops, everything and everyone was subject to scrutiny.

He was always aware of what his subordinates were up to. That was how he had rumbled that it was Sid who had made the calls.

Chapter 28

Chardonnay Takes Off

Following Fred's misguided attempts to remodel her website, influenced by his unshakeable belief in his Diamond philosophy, to update it along the lines in which he thought that it should operate, Chardonnay's eBay business came to a shuddering halt.

She had shown Fred the door and he was now living at Nick's house with Sid and Besharat.

No more chattering printers clicking into action through the night, no more packing of orders ready for the Hermes Courier to collect and deliver.

There was only Wayne and herself in the house. Together they worked to try and salvage what they could from the wreckage of her eBay business.

As she lay in bed, she pondered about how her life back in

the Lower Pennines, which had started off so brightly had suddenly turned so dark.

Her thoughts as she drifted off to sleep increasingly turned back to her old life in Spain and the factors which had encouraged her to leave it behind to return to the United Kingdom.

During the day she shifted her remaining eBay stock as best as she could door to door. At weekends she was joined on her market stall, car boot pitch and pop up sales events by Wayne who had inherited her entrepreneurial flair.

Wayne had discovered rabbits and how fast they multiplied from his Sex Education classes at school and had persuaded her to buy him a breeding pair.

The shelves that Fred had constructed for her stock were now filling up with hutches for Wayne's growing pet rabbit business. He was giving them away free to his school pals. There were so many of them.

He had also discovered plants and nature from the Forest School[47] where he had been a pupil. He put theory into practice and had taken over her back garden and allotment to grow fast growing greens to service the appetite of the local increasing rabbit population.

That was where the money was. The more rabbits you gave away, the more the demand for greens and carrots to feed them. Soon he had all the allotment holders supplying him with both and his food profits started to grow and grow.

Chardonnay didn't want to discourage Wayne. She had always been a self-starter herself. She was torn, whether to

---

[47] http://www.muddyfaces.co.uk/forest_schools.php Forest School Overview

stay in the Lower Pennines or head back to the sunshine of Spain.

It was an advert in the local newspaper for Station Managers for a budget airline which swung her decisively in favour of the sunshine option.

Its requirements described almost exactly what she had been doing in her eBay business.

Experience in customer service management in high-density environments

Able to work alone as well as handle a team and crew.

Oversee activities outdoors, which include the runways and boarding areas.

Responsibly manage their ground operations station budgets for labour, supplies and all other expenses.

A station manager working for an airline is also part customer service manager and must keep travellers satisfied and happy.

Commercial airlines fly on set schedules, and an airline station manager must ensure flights leave on time whenever safely possible.

From the job requirements, she decided that she ticked all the boxes from her previous Avon and eBay experience.

They were all transferable skills, the only thing that she lacked was product and service knowledge of commercial airline operations.

She filled in the online application form, highlighting the most relevant parts of her experience.

The invitation for interview at the airline's Manchester Airport base dropped through her letterbox a few weeks later.

Chapter 29

Chardonnay Checks In

The interview went smoothly because of the matched eBay shared skills required for the Station Manager's post.

Basically, the only area for which she required training was in airline operations and civil aviation law. She was offered and accepted a position on the training programme and agreed a start date, starting with Ramp Operations followed by a spell in Customer Service.

The big test before stepping into a Station Manager's job was in chaos management, real or contrived.

Managing chaos was a vital skill in the airline industry with the likelihood of flight delays, missing connections, planes in the wrong places, flight crew out of their permitted time limits.

It was what they were interested in at her interview.

'How did you deal with Fred crashing your eBay website?'

'Firstly, take it down and off line.

That limits both future customer dissatisfaction and your loss on mispriced products.

Secondly, fill the orders that you can fulfil, even if they are at a loss. Source as much replacement stock as you can.

Thirdly, limit the reputational damage, simply tell customers right away that there has been a computer malfunction and immediately refund.

Fourthly, if you can't continue on eBay, liquidate your stock, as I did, through other outlets. You have to draw a line under it as soon as possible.'

They were impressed by her response.

Her chaos test came out of the blue as Acting Station Manager at Tenerife North Airport.

The conveyor belt behind the check in desks broke down. She radioed engineering maintenance for immediate action and Customer Service staff to come on the floor.

Then quickly, they roped off named sections of the concourse for passengers on the Manchester, London Gatwick and Glasgow flights to drop their baggage.

Not perfect but workable for the agent ground crews' electric buggies to move luggage to the aircraft but keep the arrival luggage carousels and lanes free of obstruction.

'Not a bad start,' said the Operations Training Manager (OTM) watching her incognito, 'let's see how she handles the next test.'

The text message came up on her phone.' Catering supplies cold storage truck broken down in traffic …won't make loading.'

She had the Customer Service Advisor (CSA) check the outgoing passenger lists for pre-ordered meals marking up the vegetarian options.

Another radioed the incoming flights for their meal and drink stocks and also checked central supplies at Tenerife South Airport. Not enough time to shift supplies to Tenerife North for the current flight slots but might have to for later departures as well as overstocking scheduled incoming flights before take-off.

She quickly matched outgoing requirements with on-board stocks coming in and exchanged messages with the cabin crew and decided to strip the London Gatwick flight down to essentials and transfer the bulk of supplies to the Manchester and Glasgow flights. Still short on stocks but you sold more food and drinks on longer flights.

'Good decision,' thought the OTM, 'let's see if she'll improvise.'

He could see her checking her watch and calculating. Not enough time to send out a replacement to offload the broken down catering truck.

He saw her mark various names on the passenger lists giving instructions to a CSA who immediately called them to the desk to explain the situation, refund their prepaid meals, advising them to buy food locally to take with them and a discount voucher off alcoholic drinks on board.

'You've got a good one there, Mick,' said the OTM to his boss, 'there's a bigger margin on drink, and with the voucher, they'll probably buy plenty more of it!'

The conveyor belt behind the check in desks started back up to start freeing up the concourse floor.

Chapter 30

Jeremy Kyle before the break

Chardonnay had been so busy in training for her new job and future that the long scheduled Jeremy Kyle date with Fred suddenly rushed up on her.

The events which had led to it, her return to the Lower Pennines, followed by Fred's disastrous crashing of her eBay business now seemed so long ago in the past.

The intensity of her airline training in Station Management had put it clean out of her mind.

Her life had moved on.

She saw little of Fred, only when he took Wayne for days out, or when she had spotted him when she and Wayne were shifting her eBay stock door to door or on the local market.

They were interviewed separately at the studios in Manchester.

Both followed the same schedule with the programme's staff, questions about their relationships, their split, then getting together again after her return from Spain, only to split again after Fred had destroyed her eBay business.

There were lie detector tests which they both took and a DNA test which she had rejected along with psychological profiling.

Fred had elected to take the DNA test which he thought might be useful for his Genealogy project on tracing his ancestors.

The psychologist was interested in Fred's breakdown and diagnosis of Closed Mind syndrome and his obsession with Diamond. He slid a sheet of paper across the desk to Fred. 'What do you see there?' he said.

Fred looked at the black dots on the page and an object suddenly appeared to him.

'A triangle,' he replied, 'a white triangle.'[48]

The psychologist said, 'Look again.'

Fred looked, the white triangle had disappeared. All that was there were three black Pac Man dots.

'You have phantom vision syndrome,' he said,' have you heard of phantom limb syndrome?'

Fred shook his head as the psychologist continued, 'Phantom limb syndrome occurs when an individual continues to receive sensation or even pain signals from a limb that has been amputated.'

---

[48] Kanizsa's Triangles
https://www.google.co.uk/?gws_rd=ssl#q=Kanizsa+triangle

'Phantom vision syndrome works in the same way. A misfire in the brain that occurs in people, similar in effect to phantom limb syndrome.'

'As vision wanes, the brain continues to interpret visual imagery from stored images in the absence of any visual input and fills in the blanks, just as in the case of the phantom limb amputee, the brain sometimes continues to process pain signals from something that is no longer there.'

'That is where your obsession with Diamond comes from. Because it may work well in one environment, doesn't necessarily mean, that it will work well in another.'

Fred's certainties about life were being jolted again.

Finally, both he and Chardonnay were seated down on the set for filming to start. Fred noted Chardonnay's deep tan from her new airline job in the sun spots of Europe.

The host, Jeremy held both the lie detector and Fred's DNA results in his hand and started the questions.

'So let's get this going, then.'

'You both drifted apart almost as soon as you married because of Army life and its long absences, right?'

They both nodded.

'Then you Chardonnay had an affair, got pregnant and ran off with the Bingo Bingo Manager to Magaluf.'

'And you Fred had an affair with Daphne a work colleague at PASTELLS. Then you both got back together again, when Chardonnay returned from Spain, with your child Wayne, right?'

'Then you split again after you, Fred, destroyed Chardonnay's eBay website and business because of your obsession with the Army Diamond strategy.'

'Today, we're looking to see if you two can get back together again.'

'Has there ever been anyone else involved in the split? Have either of you ever had sex with anyone else apart from the Bingo Bingo Manager and Daphne?'

They both shook their heads.

'Are you sure?', the host said, holding up his notes.

'You, Fred, on your lie detector test, when you were asked the question, have you ever had sex with anyone apart from Daphne?, you said No and the lie detector test confirms that you were telling the truth.'

'You, Chardonnay, on your lie detector test, when you were asked the question, have you ever had sex with anyone apart from the Bingo Bingo Manager?, you said No and the lie detector test registers that you were lying.'

'Join us after the break for the DNA results.'

Chapter 31

Jeremy Kyle after the break

That was Fred's first shock. As they sat in their chairs, Fred's mind whirled over the past, his absences on Army Service overseas, the failed reconciliation attempt in Benidorm, Chardonnay's absence on his discharge at Catterick. He racked his brains trying to think who could have been Chardonnay's other lover.

'5,4,3,2,1 we're now back on air and … Action!' barked the Floor Manager through the ear piece.

'Welcome back to the Jeremy Kyle Show,' said the host, facing the camera, 'Before the break, the lie detector tests showed that Fred told the truth and Chardonnay lied.'

'Lie detector test results are 96% accurate!' he said.
'But that can't be true! I'd have known about it,' protested Fred, as Chardonnay averted her gaze.

'So you're one of the 4% are you, Chardonnay?' shouted the host, directly confronting her in her chair.

'We also offered both parties DNA tests. Chardonnay refused, Fred accepted and I have here in my hand Fred's DNA result.'

Flourishing the paper he said, 'The DNA test shows that Fred is not the father of Wayne.'

That was Fred's second shock.

His mind in turmoil and shock about Chardonnay's unknown other lover and the thunderbolt that Wayne was not his son sent it into overdrive.

Who was her lover? Who was Wayne's father? He thought about Wayne and his blagging skills on selling Chardonnay's eBay stock door to door and his new venture of breeding rabbits to give away and racking in the cash from selling green and root vegetables to feed them.

He racked his brains and suddenly all these images and questions in his mind came together. It had to be someone in Special Ops. Only someone in Special Ops would know about his marital problems, his failed reconciliation in Benidorm but who? It all suddenly clicked together.

It had to be Sid, his best man, his Army colleague, his work colleague at SuperStore, his reputation as a womaniser and a blagger.

His turmoil turned to anger and in a rage he stood up to stride over to Chardonnay to confront her.

'EXCUSE ME, FRED!,' shouted the host,' this is MY show, that's MY name, Jeremy Kyle, on the wall, NOT Fred the Spread, so why don't you sit down, shut up, and let me talk. Yeah?'

Security grabbed Fred and in a tight clinch escorted him behind the set, where he was pushed into a chair.

Sitting in deep rage and anger, a pair of tanned arms from behind him slid down his neck and chest.

He pushed them away, rose from the chair, turning to confront Chardonnay over her double betrayal.

That was Fred's third shock. It was Daphne.

His rage and anger evaporated as he gazed at the woman who had taught him so much and he'd let slip through his hands to Italy when Chardonnay had unexpectedly returned from Magaluf.

She gently took him by the hand and led him to the studio offices behind the set and sat him down. As she talked to him, Chardonnay's double betrayal started to fade from his mind and memories of how much Daphne had meant to him started to fill their place.

Daphne had finished her work on the new free course for the Open University Future Learning programme on sexual practices that she had been working on.

Her stint in the Emergency Room of the Jeremy Kyle Show was the final bit and she had renamed the course.

'I'm now going to call it Sexual Practices Down the Centuries – The road from Athens to Magaluf via the Lower Pennines and Jeremy Kyle.'

As they chatted, all the old happy memories and how well they had worked together at PASTELLS up to the disasters of the Great Day came flooding back.

The time flew past as they talked and laughed about their recent shared past.

He didn't object when she gently took him by the hand and led him to her red sports car in the studio's car park.

All of the bitterness and betrayals from the morning show with Chardonnay had faded away and receded into a distancing bad memory.

From the passenger seat he gazed in wonderment and affection at her as she swung it out of the car park entrance of Media City, past the Trafford Centre, heading off over Barton Bridge on the M60 and onward to the Lower Pennines.

Chapter 32

BREEXIT

Bert MI6 sat in the sunshine of his balcony in the Castilla Parador and checked his watch. All the balconies were tiered for both views and privacy.

Below him, he could hear the raucous good natured banter from a large party of Royal Mail workers on the balcony below. He didn't mind.

They were family men, always up very early in the morning for swimming and pool games with their kids and relatively early to bed at night after a singsong and barbecue. They had loads of barbecues.

They were challenging each other to see who could finish off the weekend big cryptic crossword in the *Sun* first.

'17 across, last one to finish, lads and I'm fully complete,' shouted one.

'What's the clue?,' shouted another.

'17 across, Football Club Chief Executive no longer going Dutch.' was the reply.

'How many letters?,' shouted another.

'Great, big bagfuls,' was the retort, to lots of in-joke laughter, 'Seriously, lads , it's dead easy and simple, it's (2,8).'

'Gotta be Ed Woodward[49],' shouted another.

---

[49] Joint Chief Executive of Manchester United.

He smiled to himself as awaited the loves of his life. Their flight was due to arrive in less than two hours.

Their banter reminded him of his own group background in Special Ops in a totally different environment, much smaller but the same type of group shared humour.

From his balcony he could see his vision on how the development of the Canaries should come about in the future start to rise from the ocean. The lift shafts were almost complete. The cranes were now lifting the infill walls and floors to connect the resort together.

It was the first of its kind in Tenerife. The dust and rubble from the demolition of KETCHOUPP!!'s development in Magaluf was a distant but very profitable memory.

KETCHOUPP!! had bought it for £150,000 because of the possible illegal development question mark hanging over it though it was worth about £5m.

It was Tristram who had spotted the opportunity before it had been demolished and filed a claim. The law in Spain had been changed.

The new law, the Ley Organica del Poder Judicial (LOPJ) provided that where a property had been bought in good faith then compensation for the owner must be agreed by the Ayuntiamento before demolition can take place.

Compensation was agreed based on the market value of £5m. plus £1m for loss of trade. That plus the near £5m. from Sid's lottery win gave KETCHOUPP!! a pot of near £11m. to start the Tenerife development.

He had got the Tenerife idea from Dubai with its World of

Islands development.[50]

His development was starting to gain publicity in both the the local, national and international press.

BREEXIT (British Real Estate Excitement In Tenerife). The first islands' outlines were in the shape of Great Britain and Ireland. Soon the other islands would follow.

It was the first off shore development of its kind in the Canaries and looking at the works taking place he could visualize the finished product.

Together hand in hand with the loves of his life, Chardonnay and Wayne, they all looked out and shared his dream as he spoke and pointed out where the other countries of the world would be.

From the imperfect world he had grown up and worked in, he was now able to create his own perfect world, in miniscule.

THE END

---

[50] http:/www.privateislandsonline.com/islands/the-world-islands-dubai World of Islands

Thanks for reading this book which I hope you found enjoyable. Reviews, ratings, suggestions etc. would be greatly appreciated on both Amazon and Goodreads on the sites below:

Amazon.co.uk
Amazon.com

The review link is below the Author's name

From Helmand to Heywood Paperback – 16 Aug 2016

by Des Farry (Author)

Be the first to review this item

Goodreads.com

Insert From Helmand to Heywood in Search box . The Rating is immediately below the Front Cover Picture

THE AUTHOR

Des Farry comes originally from Northern Ireland and has been resident in Manchester for a large number of years. He has previously published or contributed to "How to" books on free air travel, taxation, corporate finance and public sector accounting. He has also written a number of short stories over the years and contributed to the Dublin Writers' Electric Acorn in the past.

20781054R00071

Printed in Great Britain
by Amazon